Hugh Miller Thompsons

The World and the Wrestlers: Personality and Responsibility

Hugh Miller Thompsons

The World and the Wrestlers: Personality and Responsibility

ISBN/EAN: 9783743321496

Manufactured in Europe, USA, Canada, Australia, Japa

Cover: Foto ©ninafisch / pixelio.de

Manufactured and distributed by brebook publishing software (www.brebook.com)

Hugh Miller Thompsons

The World and the Wrestlers: Personality and Responsibility

THE BOHLEN LECTURES FOR 1895

THE WORLD AND THE WRESTLERS

PERSONALITY AND RESPONSIBILITY

BY

HUGH MILLER THOMPSON

BISHOP OF·MISSISSIPPI

NEW YORK
THOMAS WHITTAKER
2 AND 3 BIBLE HOUSE
1895

The John Bohlen Lectureship.

John Bohlen, who died in Philadelphia on the 26th day of April, 1874, bequeathed to trustees a fund of One Hundred Thousand Dollars, to be distributed to religious and charitable objects in accordance with the well-known wishes of the testator.

By a deed of trust, executed June 2, 1875, the trustees, under the will of Mr. Bohlen, transferred and paid over to "The Rector, Church Wardens, and Vestrymen of the Church of the Holy Trinity, Philadelphia," in trust, a sum of money for certain designated purposes, out of which fund the sum of Ten Thousand Dollars was set apart for the endowment of The John Bohlen Lectureship, upon the following terms and conditions:

"The money shall be invested in good substantial and safe securities, and held in trust for a fund to be called The John Bohlen Lectureship, and the income shall be applied annually to the payment of a qualified person, whether clergyman or layman, for the delivery and publication of at least one hundred copies of two or more lecture sermons. These lectures shall be delivered at such time and place, in the city of Philadelphia, as the persons nominated to appoint the lecturer shall from time to time determine, giving at least six months' notice to the person appointed to deliver the same, when the same may conveniently be done, and in no case selecting the same person as lecturer a second time within a period of five years. The payment shall be made to said lecturer, after the lectures have been printed and received by the trustees, of all the income for the year derived from said fund, after defraying the expense of printing the lectures and the other incidental expenses attending the same.

"The subject of such lectures shall be such as is within the terms set forth in the will of the Rev. John Bampton, for the delivery of what are known as the 'Bampton Lectures,' at Oxford, or any other subject distinctively connected with or relating to the Christian Religion.

"The lecturer shall be appointed annually in the month of May, or as soon thereafter as can conveniently be done, by the persons who for the time being shall hold the offices of Bishop of the Protestant Episcopal Church of the Diocese in which is the Church of the Holy Trinity; the Rector of said Church; the Professor of Biblical Learning, the Professor of Systematic Divinity, and the Professor of Ecclesiastical History, in the Divinity School of the Protestant Episcopal Church in Philadelphia.

"In case either of said offices are vacant, the others may nominate the lecturer."

Under this trust, the Right Rev. HUGH MILLER THOMPSON, D.D., D.C.L., Bishop of the Diocese of Mississippi, was appointed to deliver the lectures for the year 1895.

CONTENTS.

LECTURE	PAGE
I. Personality of Man	5
II. Personality of God	45
III. Responsibility of God	79
IV. Responsibility of Man	111

LECTURE I.

PERSONALITY OF MAN.

And Jacob was left alone; and there wrestled a Man with him until the breaking of the day. And when He saw that He prevailed not against him, He touched the hollow of his thigh; and the hollow of Jacob's thigh was out of joint, as he wrestled with Him. And He said, Let Me go, for the day breaketh. And he said, I will not let Thee go, except Thou bless me. And He said unto him, What is thy name? And he said, Jacob. And He said, Thy name shall be called no more Jacob, but Israel: for as a prince hast thou power with God and with men, and hast prevailed. And Jacob asked Him, and said, Tell me, I pray Thee, Thy name. And He said, Wherefore is it that thou dost ask after My name? And He blessed him there. And Jacob called the name of the place Peniel: for I have seen God face to face, and my life is preserved.

GEN. xxxii. 24–30.

THE WORLD AND THE WRESTLERS.

LECTURE I.

PERSONALITY OF MAN.

IT is my purpose in these Lectures—the duty of delivering which I have accepted with great diffidence—I will not say to discuss, I will much less say to explain, but to call attention to, and make suggestions upon, the fact of Personality, which is to me the most wonderful fact in my knowledge—I think, indeed, I may say in the whole circle of human knowledge.

That I say "I"; that I speak to other "I's"; that I deal with them, meet them, talk to them, love some of them more than I love myself; that some of them have gone from my sight; that I have stood by the graves where we buried their material forms, and yet that they are living to me; will, indeed, never die to me; are more living and more dear and near to me than other "I's" which are full of what we call life and action—these things, I say, which are *facts*, and to me, at least, are far more wonderful and closely important facts than any others, must be, like other facts, accepted and dealt with.

They are practically excluded from the circle of what, in our day, is called Science, which has taken for herself as yet a very narrow range.

The science of man is not biology, nor even psychology, nor sociology. The most complete discussion of the physical make-up and bodily origin of man, the same discussion of his intellectual powers, and the added study of his social habits and conditions have not grasped the real question.

One can, for instance, study biology in oysters, in barnacles, in mosquitoes. (And the biology of these last is, in some respects, far more curious than that of man.) One can study psychology in apes. I love to study it in dogs, and in them it is wonderful. One can study sociology in bees, and devote a well-spent life to it; and one might —which nobody has yet done—devote a life to the study of sociology in ants, with great profit, perhaps, certainly with great interest to himself and others. But none of these sciences touch at all the questions I have suggested.

Shall we go on excluding from Science the most close, pressing, experienced facts with which we are familiar? How comes the "I"? What does it mean to be an "I" and say "I"? to stand by itself and separate itself from the entire universe completely; yes, *completely*, and just as completely from all other "I's"? How comes it to feel that it can stand alone, *must* stand alone, indeed, very often, and assert itself in the teeth of all circumstances and of all men, and say, "I will," or "I will not"? How comes it most insolently, in one point of view, to stand before ten thousand other "I's" and say in their scowling faces, "This ought to be," "This ought *not* to be;" "I will die, but I will stand by it, that this is wrong" or "this is right"? How comes this?

Shall we ever have a branch of Science called "pneumatology"? Science has never reached the pneuma yet. Hitherto she has dealt with men as animals, somata, psychai, bodies, living things—bodies in their biology: the way they live and continue their kind; science of vegetables, of cabbages and carrots; science of cholera germs, diphtheria, and smallpox.

With psychology, in a way: what sense the things and creatures have; how they manage to keep up the psyche, the life, the arrangements and provisions for existence and continuance.

With sociology also: how the things and creatures live together and repel and attract each other; the sociology of cucumbers and squashes, which every gardener ought to know or he will spoil both crops. Indeed, a step farther, rising even to ourselves—a vast stride; that higher races and lower races of men, both living together in equal conditions, must strike a general average, and the high must go half-way down if the low is to come half-way up.

But with pneumatology Science bows herself out. I believe Science is wrong by her own definition of herself. Why should she leave the pneuma to religion alone? Why abandon it in despair to what some of her disciples consider the dreams and imaginations of mere religion?

There are the *facts!*—facts evident, insistent, close about our paths and about our beds; facts of the "I" and its duties, its transgressions and their penalties, its days and its nights, its companionships and its loneliness, its awful experiences, its visions of the high, white heavens and of the awful, low-down, lurid hells. *Why has Science walled all these facts out?*

Will you pardon me for saying that I think Science is very small so far? Small, because she ignores the facts right at her door, puts on her spectacles, and goes round, like an ancient witch, in the dark and the swamp, to find "facts" which, if they be facts, are of no great vital consequence to men, and never deigns to deal with or help to explain the facts that stare me in the face at my hearthside, at my lying down, at my rising up.

But Science is in her childhood yet, and must grow; or, to use her own phrases, "develop" or "evolute." She has millions of long miles before her, and possibly thousands of long years, and she is creeping yet; has, perhaps, by God's blessing, in these last years, been provided with a go-cart (I hope so), that she may learn the sooner to walk —namely, the working hypothesis of evolution.

So let us be very thankful that there is any movement at all, on the line of knowing things, by the human psyche—any movement beyond trying to know how to provide the human soma with better food, drink, and shelter.

It is inevitable that, at last, there shall be some

attempt to know something of man; and that means, for us Nicene Christians, something of God. The Pneuma will seek to be known also.

For man is pneuma, and God is Pneuma. The Lord put those two facts together long ago. "God is a Spirit [Pneuma]: and they that worship Him must worship Him in spirit and in truth."

I believe there is a science of the pneuma possible, and to be formulated sometime—a collection and formulation of the *facts* concerning *egos*, *I's*—that is, men and God. These are the only I's that Science can recognize and investigate.

I think these are legitimate subjects, too, of scientific investigation; I do not mean speculative or metaphysical word-confusion, I mean *scientific* investigation upon the strictest and most peremptory lines.

It will take many ages, perhaps, before Science, working up through bathybius, monads, and mollusks, developing slowly, as the law of development compels, will venture upon the study of an "I" even finite and earthly, and all the facts that "I" holds, and all that grow out of them.

It will take, no doubt, endless myriads of ages, and in other worlds, before Science reaches the point of trying to study and understand the awful, infinite, eternal "I Am that I Am." And yet "to know God, this is life eternal." But this will be science of the pneuma, not of the psyche.

I believe there is no knowing man apart from knowing God. These two have always gone together—somehow are always bound together. You may know all about a horse, I think; all about a mule, even (a much more "differentiated" animal)—I was going to say, without knowing anything about God; but I doubt even that. I am sure you can know nothing about man, in the differentiation which makes him man and distinguishes him from either the bird or the animal, without knowing a great deal about God. You certainly cannot know much about God unless you know a good deal about man.

For these two are "I's," and, as far as we can study them in this visible world, are the only "I's." I hesitate to say it, yet why should I? In scientific speech I should be compelled to say it. In Nicene speech I say it continually. These two "I's" *are of one species!* From the one I can at least begin the study of the other. "All power is given unto Me in heaven and in earth." A Man, remember, said this. He is a Man to-day, as He was then. He will remain a Man forever.

We start with *that* and all its consequences (and they are overwhelming) as a matter of faith.

In the end it will be a matter of Science—that Man governs the universe. The end of all living, saving faith is knowledge. Faith is tentative, helps you to *scientia* at last—the outcome of faith, that for which faith was given. Faith in this realm furnishes, that is, the " working hypothesis."

I have therefore decided in these Lectures to ask you to let your thought play about the subject of Personality. It will, in the ages coming, be a subject of scientific investigation. It is, I need scarcely say, not such a subject yet, and nevertheless it lies at the basis of all Science. Unless there be an " I " to know, there can be no knowledge.

Of course I am aware that " metaphysics," as it is called, studies and has studied the ego. But I am using the word " science " here in its strict meaning—the gathering and coördinating of ascertained, visible, hearable, or tangible facts. In that sense Science has declined, so far, to deal with the " I "—much to my surprise, and your surprise, if you will consider all that the neglect implies. But, as I say again, Science is yet in the germ, and will develop into somewhat really vital as man develops and becomes more a man and more an "I."

My line is the humble one of suggesting. I have no theory. I have no science myself. I am not anxious to have you agree with me. I am desirous to set you thinking. To think is itself an end, and a great one. To think on high things is a noble end and a sufficient, whether or not you come to a logical, formulated conclusion.

Indeed, logical, formulated, walled-in, and finished conclusions on the essentials of things are sure to be false. They are only true in the counting and arranging and measuring of the outward relations of things.

For instance, you can weigh an alleged ton of coal, and come to an unerring logical and mathematical conclusion that eighteen hundred pounds is *not* a ton, although you may have paid for a ton!

But you cannot weigh a spiritual or even an intellectual force, and decide how many foot-pounds of such energy were exhausted by the dealer in cheating you out of those two hundred pounds of coal!

To say what I have to say on this subject of Personality, I make my starting-point one of the most illogical and, to the lower intelligence (the psyche of St. Paul, the invisible part we share with our dogs and horses), the most mysterious of all the incidents in the Old Testament. It appeals entirely to the pneuma, as you will see—the spiritual understanding; that which differentiates man. You cannot bring to its full understanding the psychical intelligence at all, which is nevertheless so imperative—that intelligence which the horse exercises when he goes to the watering-trough, and man exercises when he decides that one thousand dollars at ten percent. per annum is just as profitable, as an investment, as two thousand dollars at five percent. per annum, supposing the security be equally good.

The incident is outside all that, though all that lay near it, as it always does—in this case very close.

It is in the realm of the pneuma; deals with pneumata, "I's," personalities; and is discerned only in the realm of realities—the kingdom spiritual.

The incident is wholly mysterious—dark with the night and the desert silences, awful with the loneliness of the midnight stars and the empty world, burst into at the last with the red shafts of the dawn.

But the mystery throws no shadow upon the

central fact. Two "I's" are here, two "thou's," two persons.

They are at grips with each other. Each clasps, holds, strains, questions the other. There is the sense that each has a hold upon the other. The hold may be for good or for ill. But it is a wrestling hold; contains the power to question, and to lame or to bless.

One of the wrestlers we know. He is just a man, and by no means a noble or a strong man. His life has been a mean, tricky life from the beginning. He cheats his father, old and blind; he turns deaf ears to the cry of his starving brother for food. He has it, but refuses to share it save at the price he may wring from utmost need. And the brother is his twin brother, and he has already cheated him out of his father's blessing.

The man has fled from the face of the angry brother—am I wrong in saying the righteously indignant brother? All times are alike to men, since men are found the same in all times. And to take advantage of a brother's need, to traffic in his want and hunger, to forestall the market and make one's self rich out of his misery, to play upon his simplicity and trust, even play upon his weakness and his sins, is as old as brotherhood, you see.

There is nothing of this sort in our dealings in produce exchange or coal market that was not at work in this man—the supplanter.

He had bad blood in him. The law of heredity is tyrannous. He had been taught his trickery by his mother, who came by it legitimately. It is bad enough to be taught ill by one's father—to inherit evil from him. Greatly worse is it to inherit wickedness from, or be taught wickedness by, one's mother!

The serene, stately, dreamy desert prince Isaac, who walked abroad in the splendid eventides of the Orient to muse in the meadows alone, was true son of his princely father. But this wrestling, straining man, caught at last in his own evil nets, owed it to the bad strain from his beautiful mother's Mesopotamian kindred.

Nay, Science does not teach us anything that we do not read on the pages of these old *Biblia*, these books which the spiritual consciousness of the ancient children of God selected, and by that consciousness canonized, and held, by whomsoever written, edited, or revised within her, as sacred and inspired upon God's nature and man's, and the ethical relations between these two.

Evil fruit from evil seed always! Wrong working out further wrong! Bad children from bad fathers! The terrible persistence of the evil thing done, and the glorious blessing of the thing well done! The awful abiding of the *fact*, and the fruitfulness thereof forevermore!

From the face of the brother the prescient mother sent her favorite to her own kin. Somehow it always goes so. It is the ethical law. The liar goes to liars, the trickster finds himself among tricksters, the knave among knaves. One goes to his own place in this world. Shall he not go to his own place in all worlds? Even Judas has friends somewhere and finds society. He goes "to his own place."

Yet even to such an one as Jacob come, in the loneliness of the night, the visions that tell him of a loftier life and a higher order.[1] Wheresoever he comes into nature and her silences the upper realm breaks on this man strangely. "Strangely," do I say? Is it not the rule? Alone on the mountain summit, alone with the stars, alone with the sea, what does the soul not utterly gone to the other side care for flocks and herds, for stocks or bonds or bank-accounts, so only he sees once that the real eternal home lies above, and one must

[1] Gen. xxviii. 10-15.

climb, not crawl, and the long, strange ascent must be toward the everlasting light!

So what we call "nature"—which is God's expression of Himself to His child while man stays His child—calls him to worship, and in her vast aisles and naves, which we but poorly imitate in our noblest architecture, lifts him to the splendor of what lies above all summits, and the worship that chants its liturgies beyond the gold-and-purple rood-screens of all earthly dawns, where he makes the snow-crags his altars.

God walks the mountains. God dwells in the thick darkness. God speaks in the thunder, in the roar of the cataract, in league-long breakers thundering on the shore. One meets His footsteps on the loneliness of the illimitable sea, comes near Him in the vast silences of desolate lands.

The grand nature-liturgy of the old Hebrew books is reverent as it is true, fearless as it is spiritual. It is chanted from Moses to David, from David to the prophets. They all have caught the stately rhythm of the worship of the living God, who is present, ruling, working, revealing Himself in star and flower and little bird, in avalanche and ice summits, in the little rivulet singing low through the clover, in the roar of the cataract plunging from the steep.

So it came even to this man, who still remained, notwithstanding his sin, a child of Abraham, to see his vision in the desert as he fled to Padan-aram. But in the vision he saw only what he was able to see. It is thus always. The divinest vision reveals what the seer is capable of seeing. In the ladder let down from heaven, in the angels ascending and descending, he sees only what he is capable of seeing, hears only what he is capable of hearing.

The ladder, you will observe, suggests no climbing for him. The voice of the Lord from the summit has no call to a nobler life. That life has run on low levels thus far, and still, even from opened heaven, this man hears only of flocks and herds and increase and an earthly success.

And still, even so, it was much. There was a world higher than this. There was a God who could bless, and from whom one could seek good things, and who loved to give them. He was good, at least to some men, and would give them many good things and keep old promises, for He was true and righteous—so only men served and loved Him. There were steps up to Him, and messengers to come and go.

There are profound lessons in that first desert vision, though I cannot dwell upon them here.

One of them is that God necessarily meets men on the levels where they stand; that to raise them He stoops—must finally stoop to Gethsemane and the cross, indeed; and also that, with heaven opened, they have eyes to see only what they *can* see, and ears to hear only what they *can* hear.

The man rises in the morning and tries to make a bargain with Him whom he has seen in the vision. It is a pledge of so much offering and so much service for so many sheep and oxen, kine and camels. It reveals the spiritual nature at its lowest. Still it is a spiritual nature, and believes in a spiritual world above sheep and oxen.

And the man goes on his journey, and it fares with him according to the vicissitudes of an entirely earthly life.

The life for twenty years thereafter was lived on exceedingly low levels. It was a war of wits between himself and his uncle Laban; and the wives he married seem to have been true daughters of their father, and thoroughly fit for the husband.

One does not wonder that the elder brother, impetuous, imperious, princely, preferred the daughters of Heth, the princesses of the desert, to these scheming relatives of his, who could help the husband to cheat the father, and in their elopement should even rob the poor old semi-idolater of his ancestral images—fetishes, teraphim, whatever they were—on which he thought his luck depended.

It could not be that the beautiful Rachel stole them and lied about them because she put much faith in their power herself, after seeing how poorly they had served her father against the schemes of her husband. It is sad to think they must have been of silver (there was no gold in circulation in those days—no question of "bimetallism"), and that she stole them for their intrinsic value.

It is not at all, you will say, an edifying story; and certainly the family arrangements and the shrewd trickery of Padan-aram hold no example to you or me. But they hold *this*. Critics tell us to throw away these old *Biblia* because they are clearly not of God, in that they relate such doings by people asserted to be under God's special charge and benediction; that, indeed, they are *immoral* in such assertion, and unfit to be supposed the revelation of a righteous God.

I confess the strength of a part of the objection

from the standpoint of merely literary criticism, lower or higher.

Of course the *Biblia*—the collection of books—history, poetry (dramatic, idyllic, lyric, epic), law, ritual, folk-lore, prophesy—may be, and I, for one, frankly concede ought to be, from one side, treated simply as literature and nothing else—a collection of ancient books. Only one must not carry into them the ethics and opinions of this century, and criticize them on those grounds. That is not literary criticism at all. We must understand that the literary critic must remain content with his chosen occupation. He has nothing whatever to do with the ethics, the manners, or the opinions of the book he criticizes. He deals with it simply as a piece of written matter about whose age, authorship, and literary style alone he is concerned.

I think you will concede that this is not a very lofty, though it may be a necessary and very useful, business. Take an illustration. A critic who would spend his time on minute examination of the letters and words of Shakespeare's dramas, and who might even finally reach the conclusion that former editors were all wrong in the arrangement of the dramas, and that "Hamlet" was written before "Timon," and that "rare Ben Jonson" redacted

"King Lear"—that, indeed, Shakespeare did not write "Lear," "Macbeth," or "The Tempest" at all, but another man of the same name did—might be a very useful man, and, in his own opinion, imagine he had done the world service; but just as a bit of common sense and general usefulness, we would hardly call him a high critic, much less a "higher" critic than the man who taught all readers and lovers of the mass of literature we call "Shakespeare" to find subtler meanings, deeper philosophies, profounder insight into man and nature and the nature of the Lord of them both, than they had ever before seen or even suspected.

It abides with me as one of the queer, topsy-turvy puzzles that crop up outside the country of the Sphinx, that the term "Higher Criticism" should have been arrogated for themselves and conceded by others to gentlemen whose business upon a body of ancient literature begins and ends with criticizing its words and letters, and deriving thence its supposed dates and origins, and who have never set themselves by one flash of intelligence to deal with its meaning and its purpose! And this literature, mind, the unspeakably most influential, formative, commanding, and controlling literature known since time began!

I concede the usefulness of the alphabet critics; but why call them "higher critics"? Thomas à Kempis was a higher critic than all of them put together!

But to turn to the objection that these things are not of God because our higher sense condemns the actions related.

You ask, "Is Genesis inspired?" I should answer you, "Yes! Inspired! Profoundly inspired! Inspired as long as the world lasts!"

Does anybody say "invented, forged"? I ask, "Where is the inventor or forger so much an imbecile as to write out the story of this man Jacob —to go no further—and then to seriously dare tell us that this poor creature was 'chosen of God'?"

Suppose the story of Jacob and his father and grandfather an epic, invented by a poet, a sagaman, a scribe idealizing. Can you imagine such inventor writing out Jacob? You have examples in all literature, from Gautama Buddh to Tennyson's Arthur. Try Homer, try Virgil, try Milton's Satan, if you wish; can you find any sane inventor setting out his hero in such phrase and guise as Moses (or some other man of the same name) sets out Jacob?

Can you imagine any critic, from Celsus to Voltaire, who would propose to write you down their own lives—even their own lives most loftily idealized—as a permanent book of human ethics in the way Moses, or the other man, writes the story of the man whom God says He "loved"?

When your metaphysician, your philosopher, your scientist, your poet, your autobiographist, your historian, your dramatist, from Shakespeare down, gives you a hero, do they not all tell you what they think a man, a hero, a father of humanity ought, in their conception, to be—not at all what he is?

The only book that ever dared to write down men, heroes, demigods, beginners of races, fathers of ages, "friends of God" just as they were and as they are is the one book and the sole book of epic and drama true to God, because it is true to man—these *Biblia*.

The life of George Washington is a myth as it is read to-day. The life of Abraham Lincoln is fast becoming a myth. No historian has dared to tell us, or ever will dare to tell us, the real story of these two lives.

The life of Napoleon Bonaparte is getting itself republished, with the republication advertised in all the papers, as a new and more rational form of the Napoleonic myth, which it is proposed to impose on civilized consciousness in lieu of the "Sunday-school teacher and member of the Young Men's Christian Association" myth which Dr. Abbott wrote out, when I was younger, in *Harper's Magazine*, to the fatal misleading of the mind of one generation in the United States.

I mean to say no writer of the life of Washington, Lincoln, Grant, Jefferson, Bonaparte, or Wellington would dare to write the true life of any one of them, as this *Biblia* writes out the life of Abraham, Jacob, Moses, or David.

Therefore *they* are human, and therefore false. They are not inspired. An inspired story is the only true story ever written, or ever capable of being written, because written from the overworld of *fact*—just plain, bald, shameless, sometimes horrible fact. Every mere *un*-inspired writer, infidel or believer, pagan or Christian, feels it bounden on him to deny or pass over *facts*.

There is no man who would dare to put in print the life of any man, or his own life, as this most inexorable writer writes down the life of Jacob and other people, under the cold mercilessness of *fact*, which is just *revelation*—fact, the thing that is, relieved from your poor beclouded conceptions of what you think the fact ought to be, or even now might be, if eternal God would only take your advice!

Secular history is a collection of myths. We can see that in our own experience. There is not a man who has passed from our land during even the last half-century whose real life exists in any history.

As soon as even a small member of our Congress is dead, his fellow-members hold a session over him, and a half-dozen gentlemen elocutionize about him and formulate a *mythus officialis!* Of course, being a small person, the myth-faith extends only, as a rule, to his wife and children; and they, in spite of their own knowledge that he was small—very small indeed—accept and are delighted with the myth, and make it a part of their household worship.

That is the way myths are made. In fact, as far as my personal experience and knowledge go, I should say that, by account of writers and biographers, gentlemen whom I have known—and some of them intimately—have never existed on this earth at all; and that those I thought I knew best were shadowy ghosts waving white arms on misty mountain summits in some far land to which no man has ever gone, and from which (it might be inferred) no man has ever come.

The only hard, practical, unmythical history or biography in all literature is contained in these old *Biblia* the church holds "inspired."

So the hero Jacob has all his life told out no concealment, no reticence, no invented or stolen pretty story like that about George Washington and his hatchet; no glossing over of his sins or his family's sins.

At this time he is on his way returning to his own land under what he chooses to consider the commandment of God.

It is not in his day only that men think their own desires, or what looks like their own profit, is the commandment of God!

Numbers of us, and, curiously, the more pious of us, always are apt to hold our own decisions for the commandment of God. Especially when we have prayed over the matter, and asked for light, we are very sure we have that commandment!

I was once consulted by a gentleman who was greatly troubled in his mind, almost to the brink of black doubt, because in a change he meant to make in his business he had made the subject a matter, as he told me, of earnest prayer, and he was clear, after that, that it was God's will that he make the change, and behold, the change had resulted in the loss of half his fortune! He was very much annoyed about it—even somewhat indignant with God about it!

I suggested that the Lord had left him, in all that kind of action, to decide for himself, having given him presumable sense, and allowed him a tolerable education and some experience in his special business; and that if I were in his place I would not be angry with the Almighty because He declined to go into the wholesale grocery business with me for money in another part of the country.

I have no doubt of this man Jacob's sincerity. That is all the record vouches for. He believed he was commanded, and therefore, as far as he was concerned, having a conscience illuminated up to its capacities, he *was* commanded to return to his kindred and his father's house. But he has some lessons to learn, which will split that very poor conscience wider open before he is much older. Esau, the wronged brother, has to be met and settled with somehow. Every wrong done has to be settled at the last!

So, as he approaches the border of the land toward which he travels, he sends messengers to the brother. The brother has prospered, in his way, too. Those outside "the covenant" prosper, as this world goes, observe, as well as those inside. The elder brother has taken his own line, and he is what we would call now a Bedouin chief and a man of considerable consequence. He can march at the head of four hundred armed men! A very important brother if one have played the knave with him!

He had chosen his course also; the man of the fields, the desert, and the mountains; the hunter, the warrior, the desert prince—driven from home by the mother who could not understand and never loved her strong, rude, but tender elder son, with the old fiery Abrahamic blood in him—he too had prospered, and he was coming to meet the brother who had cheated him and mocked his father's blindness and age.

Angry? I should think so! The desert prince comes to meet the fawning, intriguing, smooth-tongued brother who had chosen flocks and herds instead of honor and manliness, and had cheated him out of his highest, if only his ideal, possession.

So Jacob prays again; thanks God for his success: "With my staff I passed over this Jordan; and now I am become two bands"—makes God, that is, the partner in all his knavery with Laban, and thanks Him that He has helped his trickery to a great fortune!

Is it all passed away? I think I have heard gentlemen thanking God for the success already attained, and praying for further success—pious gentlemen, who paid tithes even—and who honestly believed that they and their knavish ways were under direct protection and direction of Almighty God because they decorously attended church and paid their pew-rents.

The Old Testament is still a part of the revelation—an essential part. We cannot dispense with it, even if Moses did *not* write this particular book, nor Isaiah that special chapter. It is such a particularly close, practical, revealing book! Such a true-to-man book, and therefore such a true-to-God book!

The character of the younger son of Isaac remains such a genuine character, for four thousand years, of religious people, and of prosperous men "chosen of God," that, having been true for so many centuries, and nobody disputing the fact that it is true now, I am, as it were, obliged to believe that no popular novel-writer in an illustrated magazine of ancient Syria could have invented it! There is no human experience that makes such *writers* possible. All human experience makes the *character* possible, permanent, familiar, and all alive with us now.

The man's arrangements to meet his wronged and outraged brother are entirely natural from his character. He sends "presents" before him. The desert free-lances are always hungry. They have been hungry for four thousand years! The sheep and cattle will appease him. Three cattle-droves with herdsmen, all to repeat the same abject lie, "A present for my lord Esau, from his servant Jacob," are to meet the chief and his hungry horde. The capitalist Jacob offers that kind of blackmail which capital, in its supreme need, will always abjectly pay to dinnerless force. The world is a very young world after all—in its babyhood, I think. We have scarce advanced in very vital things for forty centuries.

The capitalist was a coward—we say still that "capital is timid." The capitalist himself is timid, fearful, cowardly. Several of them have voluntarily exiled themselves in these last years from our own peaceful, happy, and prosperous land.

When blackmail must be paid it is a very shaking time for the capitalist, and this man of ours is scared. He is worse—he is an abject coward. He sends his presents before him, then his cattle and servants, then his wives and children.

The story is a very pitiful one. The whole conduct of the man is unmanly, fawning, mean, and lying—the only kind of bearing which wealth in the last battle can oppose to force. It is all very low.

When all had passed over the ford of the brook Jabbok, this man remained alone, far from the danger before him.

The night was one of fear and trembling. "Jacob was left alone." His cowardice compelled him to be alone. Once again in the silences, once more under the watching stars! The old memories come back to him: the tent of his father; the sports of his boyhood, the face of the brother he had loved and with whom he had shared them; his beautiful mother's eyes upon them both; his stately father's presence, serene always, and always princely, whom now, tottering under his century of wintry years, he is soon to meet. He and the brother he had wronged alone left to close the eyes of the blind chieftain of their race, and they, wronger and wronged! They two alone in all the world of the legitimate seed of the great prince and sage—"the friend of God."

It was an hour of heart-searching for this man. Flocks, herds, servants, family—all his wealth might have already vanished before the wild children of the waste and their fierce lord, for aught he knew, and he left, as when he fled a score of years before.

Conscience comes to close quarters with a man at such a time. Jacob's conscience, you may be sure, was busy with him. In the few strong strokes which paint the scene this lies outlined. The worth of his life, its hard, uncompromising reality, comes to him. He takes stock of himself. It is in such supreme moments that a man is compelled to weigh his own worth and the worth of his life. In the dark of the world he *sees*, in the silence of the loneliness he *hears*.

But a man, in the hour that shakes his soul to its center, has not alone his own conscience to deal with. "God is greater than our heart, and knoweth all things." Settle with myself as I may, how shall I settle with another? There is immanent in conscience another Man, a strange Man, not myself, not any other man I ever knew;

awful, singular, lonely, and yet persistently near. I must also settle with *Him!*

"What shall I do then with Jesus which is called Christ?" cried Pilate, in mortal terror, ages after this. "What shall I do with this strange Man, who comes and goes about me and about my fathers, who is the eternal measure and rule of righteousness? How stand I with Him, and what shall I say to Him?"

It is the mystic question heard on all the winds of Palestina, heard in all the solemn silences of time. This Man, immanent, present at any hour, shadowy in dreams, plain at Abraham's tent-door, forever ready to judge, forever ready to help! The eternal presence of this Man walks the hills of the world in these old *Biblia!*

And He is here on Peniel. "There wrestles a Man with him until the breaking of the day."

It is grim and awful to come to grips with this Man. But the lonely man is going to have it out once for all. The hour is a supreme hour. Here and henceforth it must be blessing or cursing.

"Let Me go, for the day breaketh," cries the Wrestler. Already the lances of the sun flash red upon the hills. The night-fears, and the wrestle of lonely self-examination, and the bitterness of silence with one's own soul will fade into the cares and fears of the breaking day. "Let Me go."

The man must have grown wonderfully. He is changing fast. Already he is lame. The strange midnight Antagonist has touched him. He is branded, and shall stay branded all his life. Yet, "I will not let Thee go, except Thou bless me!" "What is thy name?" Mark the question. A name describes. In old days they were always given to describe, to reveal character, to tell what the man, the animal, or the thing is in its utmost purpose and meaning. This man's name did reveal. His name rang true. "He said, Jacob"—supplanter, knave, defrauder, cheat!

And then clangs out to the rising dawn and the crimson spears of the hosts of the morning the blessing: "Thy name shall be called no more Jacob, but Israel"—*prince of God!* Let the new day hear the new name. "The night is far spent, the day is at hand."

All the long night of the ages man has wrestled with the awful, eternal, omnipotent Man—wrestled undismayed, with straining limbs and palpitating muscles and throbbing heart, all the night of doubt and fear, of pain of memory and stings of conscience.

Lamed by the mighty touch, branded forever by the finger of the awful Wrestler they have dared to grasp; yet because He is a Man they have wrestled on, and behold, the cry tingles to the fleeing starlight of time, and peals in the vast halls of the abiding morning, "Thy name is prince of God"!

I am not going to attack, sneer at, or despise my own day. It is good enough for me and you —perhaps better than we deserve. But I should sneer at it and belittle it, and tell it to go about its wretched business and betake itself to the limbo of all things forgotten in any sane universe, if I believed it for one moment to be only what its current talk and writing makes it.

Man must have his Mahanaims, where the angels of God meet him. He must have his Peniels, where he meets God face to face and lives. He must have his nights of wrestling, and bear the brand of the awful touch burned into him body and soul, or he has not reached man's station in this world—the place God has prepared for him.

And mark: to get that—there is no vagueness about it—he must *tell his name*. The small personality, the finite individuality, has its own abiding permanence, and must stand by itself, endure toil, weep and rejoice by itself.

The secret of the burden and sorrow of our years is that we must say "I."

No wonder the poor Buddhist prays for *Nirvana* —just to drop into the infinite ocean and be lost, and leave all oughts and responsibilities behind one forevermore!

But this terrible religion of the Old Testament and the New keeps on, as it has kept on for all these awful centuries of human story, insisting on the "I." "What is thy name?" What is thy meaning? What is thy character? What art thou doing? Naming men, individualizing men out of all combinations and associations, insisting on the individual, and demanding that the individual shall answer for himself.

I do not know in what personality consists. I am aware that many philosophers think they do know and could make their knowledge clear to me were it not for my own stupidity. I regret that stupidity profoundly. But it is not so great as to conceal from me this: that personality is the most wonderful and awful thing in this whole universe, as far as I can see; and that while I know as little about its essence as I do about the essence of anything else, the personality, the I-ism, of the beggar is a loftier thing than Chimborazo, and a more beautiful and terrible thing than Niagara with all its thunder and its foam.

I know, too, that it is in the eclipse, in the hour of destiny and the dark, that the personality stands most sharply cut in white or black, and that the terrible " I " paints itself upon the heavens in glory or in shame.

For the world is an awful world after all. No man would ever have been fool enough to live in it, I think, if he had been given the choice.

It is a dreadful, just, far-searching, and testing world, where no tares will, under any supposition, produce wheat, and no thistles bear grapes.

And this, not because it is itself unchangeable— for it spins like a top through measureless space —but because there are " I's " upon it which are not of it, which amid its changes are changeless, amid its passings permanent, and amid its deaths immortal; and who, amid its harvests of a summer, sow and reap the sheaves of eternity!

And rising from all its voices, of the night or the busy day, of the moaning tides or the soughing forests, of the wind in the long prairie-grass or the roar of burning pine-woods, in the cry of the panther watching on the bending bough or the song of the thrush in the thicket—from all voices of star and sea and woodland comes the question to this strange wayfarer whom none know, "What is thy name?" Nature presses him with his personality; torments him with it; allows him not for one moment to forget it while he wakes; profanes his very rest in sleep, and whispers or thunders in his dreams to scare: "Yes, thou art an 'I.' What is thy name?"

Well, we might even endure what we call nature! But there is no end. We ourselves cry to ourselves, "What is thy name?" And we are dimly conscious that there is somewhere and somehow a Power behind all powers, out of space, out of time, but immanent and abiding near by our side, who, at any hour of day or night, in blessing or in life-and-death wrestle, may demand, "What is thy name?" The consciousness of their relationship to the Powers unseen, gross as it may be among some, crude as it is among all, is a fact universal among all who say "I."

But that this Power is a Person, and this relationship so close that it takes the form of clasping hands and straining arms and laboring muscles in the wrestle for life and lifting, for princedom and for crowning, which can come only in the dawning of a new day—this is the conviction which scorches the human wrestler with its touch of fire, brands him with the brand of the infinite and eternal Personality which declares him His own; in the doctrine of Divine Evolution, a prince and son of God!

LECTURE II.

PERSONALITY OF GOD.

Wherefore is it that thou dost ask after My name?
GEN. xxxii. 29.

LECTURE II.

PERSONALITY OF GOD.

THE prayer was natural. Jacob had given his own name. Why should he not know, also, the name of this strange Antagonist? That He was from beyond the world was clear. Some Power, some Existence from outside the common experience and life of men had been wrestling with him, had branded him, lamed him, at last blessed him, and made him a prince of God. That the Man was no man of his measure Jacob was sure without an answer.

For he calls the name of the place *Peniel*—" the face of God," the face of one of the Elohim he had looked upon and yet lived.

But what was His name? The inmost character, nature, and personality—what was that? That He was a Person there was no question. Jacob was sure of that. And he got no answer. Virtually it is, "How does My name concern thee? Why askest thou after *My* name?"

And this night's question has been the question of humanity always. Jacob spoke for all men and all times.

For in the night of the years, on the lonely plains of time, some Power, strange and awful, some gigantic Force with suggested human or celestial semblance, has been wrestling for good or ill with men.

In the long years of bitter struggle in which men have been straining toward the dawn, some Power beyond their own, beyond anything from the earth, has grasped them, dragged them, gripped them, to lame or to bless; and in the agony of the wrestle the passionate cry has tingled to the darkened skies, "Tell me, I pray Thee, Thy name."

Who is it that governs the earth and men, and conducts the processes of the years? For our strength avails not, nor our riches, nor our wisdom. Still the world is an awful place and our life has awful possibilities. Ruin waits upon the march of men, and ruin, many times, from the hands of brothers. Plan as we will, our plans go to wreck by the stroke of a Hand out of the darkness. Build as we will, and our towers and palaces are shivered by a blow from a Hand unseen. The mightiest growths of time in institutions, in laws, in constitutions and social order, watched, guarded, buttressed by all care, crumble under a touch we know not whence—the touch of a Hand out of the thick darkness.

The sense of the mystery that inwraps the universe; of the ever-present mystery that clothes and masters human life; of the ever-brooding Power that dwells in the dark around us, closing us into our small span—small, though it be a span of centuries—the universal sense and conviction, which may verify itself by all experience till the instinct is confirmed by the calmness of a rational judgment, makes atheism impossible.

It is no longer a question of a Power that rules, do what we will, do what all men will.

Outside there in the dark lies Power. Power that whirls the generations onward as the cataract whirls the brown leaves in the rushing November spate—*that* all men, savage, civilized, ignorant or wise, feel to the marrow of their bones.

You may gather in one congress the statesman-like wisdom and controlling guidance of the earth, and the wisest-laid plan formulated and decided upon, every man present knows, and every thoughtful man besides knows, may be blown like a thistle-down upon the wind that rises and rushes onward from the awful hills where the unseen Powers drive their chariots of the dark or the dawn.

"The wisdom of this world is foolishness with God." "He taketh the wise in their own craftiness." He charges the loftiest imaginable intelligence with folly. The old Hebrew speech carries the conviction of the ages.

No, it is not a question of a Power straining and wrestling with human nature from the beginning, and branding or blessing it. There has not been a race of men discovered yet that has made any question of such a Power. And we may be sure that the higher the race climbs, the farther its outlook over the loneliness, the more it will confess the insistence and persistence of this Power.

It is only in the effervescence of early youth, conceited with its discoveries and its rapid gains, that men have for one half-intoxicated hour dreamed that they could rule alone and gain the daybreak without the wrestle!

Such a wild hour came, and naturally very early —before the Flood—when there were giants upon the earth, and a whole new world lay open for the conquest of the race in its prime. God had turned them loose to conquer; and they conquered—those demigods of the elder day—in a way of whose magnificence we can scarcely dream, I think, while we find the mighty ruins of their glory underlying our oldest civilizations. But the Power they had forgotten, in the long reaches of human life and human triumph, lay yet behind, and the unseen Forces burst upon the earth in its profoundest security, and "swept them all away." The story of the Flood has deeper meanings in it, I think, than any likely to emerge in the mere physical discussions about it—meanings which will yet flash, I doubt not, into light and leading, as truths abiding forever in an ethical world.

No, the question is not about the existence of the Power. It is about its nature and its meaning. "Tell me Thy name."

It is a present, living cry to-day in every living land of living men. It lies at the base of all questions, and is the first demand of all thinking. All philosophies, all religions, all governments and social life, all laws, all business among men, have their rise out of this demand—as old as man, as abiding as time, perhaps as eternal as eternity.

For it means, "Tell me the world's meaning; tell me mine own. Tell me life's purpose, and death's. Tell me what time is, and eternity; what right is, and wrong; what truth is, and lies. Tell me what heaven is, and hell!"

For to know the Master of the universe, the Power that lies behind all power and that builds and destroys as it will, is to tell man all things, that he may give names like the Son of God.

It is no cry of curiosity only. It comes less from the intellect than from the heart. God pity the man who has only seen in it a question of philosophy for his study and his metaphysics! That men do so treat it is one of the most pitiable things I know in the story of human intelligence. It never has gotten an answer, put as a curious question, and it never will. "By searching canst thou find out God?"—by search of intellect, the same curious search that finds out the nature and gives the name to a beetle!

I say it is humanity's cry. But not out of its brain, not from its study. It is a cry, a passionate prayer, to the dark and the dawn, to the night on which the blood-red banners of the unknown day are even now advancing, from the knees, from the lamed and worn wrestler in the midnight mystery, half-dream, half-waking, of time—a pitiful cry and a prayer: "Tell me Thy name."

Art Thou good? Art Thou evil? Art Thou

neither? Art Thou good to-day, evil to-morrow? Blessest Thou by night, cursest Thou by day?

From the trampled battle-plain, where the dying moan and the dead look with blind eyes to a dumb heaven—"Tell me Thy name." From a city wrecked by fire, and gutters reeking with blood —"Tell me Thy name."

From cities rich and fair, where stately homes mock the splendors and the ease of the barbaric kings of old; where also the starving mother holds to her dying heart for warmth the freezing child, that shall be found dead there in the morning— "Tell me Thy name." From Christian cities where fifty thousand dollars a year is counted respectable poverty, and where men and women starve in hovels notwithstanding, and children grow up half human in noisome filth and hopeless misery, not man only, but the overlooking angels, with angelic tears, cry, "Tell me Thy name."

When the land waves yellow with its bending harvests, and the summer light sleeps golden in the orchards and the woodlands; when the happy homes of men stand thick over all the happy land, one answers the cry. It is a lovely world; the birds sing in the branches, the bees hum in the flowers, the white sails glimmer from light to dark along the brimming river, the harvestman sings as he gathers in, the sun sinks from a happy day, the yellow moon throws up her golden shield upon the breast of a happy night—" Tell me Thy name."

The answer seems easy: " Thy name is goodness."

But look again. The floods are out! The harvests are whirled away! Down the flood rush the results of the summer's toil in mingled ruin of homes and barns and stacks, of beasts and cattle; and the valley is a desolation.

There is something still to come. The bodies of men and women and little children swirl down in the whirling flood. " Tell me Thy name *now*."

Oh, so many homes of men! So many happy homes of happy men! The shouts of children in the streets! The rose-grown cottage door! The stately mansion amid its gardens and its greenery! The cry of sailors in the ships! The clank of hammers and the hum of wheels! The cheerful faces in the sunny streets! The friendly words from lips of friends! The lighted windows in the gloaming! The music through the open doors! The happy moon and stars looking down on all! " Tell me Thy name."

Behold, the bells toll, the death-cart rumbles

through the silent streets, the diggers dig hasty graves! The cottage door, the palace door, wear crape. Under the brazen sunlight, under the pitiless moonlight, the pestilence is abroad, and Death reaps his awful harvest. "Tell me Thy name."

It is, I have said, an awful world, and a terrible life, take it at its best. A few days of shine, many days of gray clouds and rain. A little fairness of balmy mornings, many storms of lashing sleet and freezing hail. Out of the dark, into the dark again, and our poor little story is told, and the world of living men knows our names no more.

There is a possibility of what is called "optimism." That the possibility of the blackest "pessimism" lives beside it has overwhelming and shocking evidence in the self-destroyers, who seek by their own hands to escape the hell of this present life, at the risk of the hell of any other.

The years grow more serious as they go on. A boy dances along the road one morning gaily enough. How sweet a thing just to be alive! A man sits by a desolate hearth one night, and the eyes of the boy, his first-born and his pride, are closed forever on this earth in the room beyond. The leaping feet lie pale and still and ice-cold side by side. He has tried all human skill. He has used all resources of knowledge and wealth. He is a man who believes in God, too, and he has prayed for the life that has gone. He has wrestled with God for it. You tell him he must submit. Of course he must! His pastor comes and tells him he *ought* to submit. Ah, that is quite another matter!

He is down among the grim things of life's utter loneliness—the old gaunt, gray, ancient questions which man has found ever new since his first child lay dead. Conventionalities count for little. Do you wonder he cries out in the night the old cry of humanity? The beggar's boy is living; the little barefoot gutter-snipe runs by his door. The ragged little wretches will throng to see the show when his son is carried out to-morrow. He is a reticent American—one of the race that "always grimly accepts the inevitable." His eyes are dry. He will sustain calmly to-morrow the drooping figure of his boy's mother in decorous fashion, as becomes him. He will return the day after to his office, and seat himself as usual at his business, and give no sign. But to-night and to-morrow night and many a lonely night thereafter the cry rings all the more terribly out of the dark of his silent and lonely wrestle, "Tell me Thy name." "What kind of Power is it—good or bad, divine or diabolic—that has gotten me and my life in its pitiless grasp?"

But it is not merely loss of one's dearest, the sore pain and bitterness of life which comes from outside a man, even from his nearest.

The awful endowment of personality needs not for its profoundest, grimmest wrestling-pain any stroke from without.

A man sits alone with himself. He needs no coffined form of dearest child or tenderest wife or heart's close brother across the threshold. He is sufficient to himself when he enters the awful chambers of darkness, where his own past, his own present, his very self sit down beside him and question him.

God help the poor, starved, cowardly, aborted "I" who has not gone off alone, with the coffined dead of his own murdered resolutions, the living ghosts of his own sins and failures, and has not dared to look the ghastly dead and the ghastly living squarely in the face!

Where the "I" is strongest, where the "name" is answered to the call and question most emphatically, there only is the darkness darkest, and the awfulness most awful, in the wrestle that breaks the bones and blasts the sinews.

There have been men who have made repentances not to be repented of; men who have had opened to them in the lonely dark the lurid fires of God's and nature's and our own poor world's everlasting wrath against the base, the foul, the false!

Yes, there have been true repentances, true wrestlings with conscience and the eternal verities, "when the wickedness of a man's heels have compassed him about;" when not man's judgment, but eternal God's has blasted him; when he has cried in agony to the awful Power that gripped the heart of him, "Tell me Thy name."

Man's judgment, man's law, man's conventionalities, man's praise or blame—what are these with the Power that has strode out of the everlasting shadow where the realities hide, straining me in His terrible hands! My poor conceits, my wretched speculations about religion, my sentimental woes, and my childish whinings because God has not explained to my babyishness the mysteries of His universe—where are these, and what, when the smoky darkness of the awful night is lit only by lurid faces that grotesquely mock my own, and while the overshadowing Power holds me, accuses me of all I have been and all I am, and my own conscience records the accusation, and the awful whisper moans out of the night, ἁμαρτημα ἀιωνιον.

Possible? Yes, possible—" eternal sin."

To the soul who has gone through such wrestle, what wretched babble must much of our religious literature, and our preachings and supposed defenses of the faith, be!

Let us be thankful if we ourselves have not wrestled on the brink of eternal hells and looked into the rolling waves of eternal sorrow. But men have so wrestled, men are so wrestling now; and there is an awful grotesqueness in hearing your lily-handed, dilettante preacher gesticulate and elocutionize his charming platitudes melodiously—a boy, perhaps, who has never known a sorrow or a repentance—for the edification of men who have wrestled with the eternal Powers on the brink of the eternal fires, for life, for help, at cost of branded, limping body and limping soul, that they may escape[1] ἁμαρτημα ἀιωνιον.

The answer to the cry in Jacob's case was, "Wherefore is it that thou dost ask after My name?" No reply came, no explanation. Has any man, to his intensest prayer, ever yet received an answer?

[1] Mark iii. 29.

Our library shelves are filled with a mass of so-called Natural Theology grown utterly meaningless.

The men who wrote on Natural Religion, and made Christianity a supplement or an extension, had clearly never wrestled.

They were dealing with questions of the intellect alone. There is, indeed, a Natural Theology in revelation. "The heavens declare the glory of God; and the firmament showeth His handiwork." But the heavens declare and the firmament shows only to him who already believes in God, and that He has a glory and has a handiwork.

By no possible examination, by no closest study of what we call "nature" can the human intellect answer the prayer, "Tell me Thy name."

Is "the Power behind phenomena" a name? All men have acknowledged a Power behind phenomena. But is that Power's name Terror or Joy? Is it Wrath or Pity? Is it conscious of itself or not? Is it merely electricity? Has it any moral quality whatever? Has it a Personal Name?

And if our speculations on the phenomena of nature give us no answer, shall it profit us to turn to the metaphysicians—the human spiders who spin out of themselves those vast webs of words, the words themselves used in arbitrary senses, which tangle up the intellect in a confusion like madness, each filmy thread promising to lead the searcher out of the tangle into light, while he creeps round and round an endless labyrinth of artificial phrase? The "ego" and the "non-ego," the "absolute" and the "related," the "unknowable" and the "conditioned"! Through what a maze have men groped since the vortices of Descartes even to our day, finding only words!

And what have they reached? The knowledge or the name of the Powers that wrestle with humanity? Is He one or many? Has He an independent existence at all? Is He conscious of Himself, if He be a self, or does He make Himself conscious only in His creation? Can we know Him, or does He even know Himself, except in us?

The wild insanity which makes men think the finite can define the Infinite, that the human intellect which does not understand what itself is can construct and define the Eternal, creeps even into theology that claims to be revealed, and puts down its shallow conclusions as eternal verities.

Take our First Article of the Thirty-nine. It undertakes to define God philosophically in poor babbling speech; to give us the definition of His character and nature—reverently done, of course, by reverent Christian men; and yet see where it lands us: "He is without body, parts, or passions." That is merely, you see, the definition of what men think God *ought* to be, what they have decided He must be out of their own thinking. Go on! Take the Second Article, wherein God tells for Himself some little about Himself. This Being, "without body, parts, or passions," has a Son, "very God, of one substance with the Father," who *has* a body, even a human body, with all its passions, hunger, thirst, weakness, and who suffers "the passion" of death by crucifixion. That is God's account about Himself.

For unless He tell us His name we cannot find it. And from the first, as here with the wrestling Jacob, to know or hear His name we must get down and ask *Him;* ask Him praying, "Tell me, I *pray Thee*, Thy name."

We here are all agreed as to one name of this midnight Wrestler. We recognize Him across forty centuries by that name, and yet, strangely enough, it is a name no man has ever uttered, and of which no man knows the syllables.

There are, in various places of Old Testament

story, accounts of the appearance upon the scene, and always to deal with men, of a Man who speaks, acts as a man, and at the last by a sudden revelation and conviction (as was long after the case at Emmaus, when the two disciples recognized Him and He vanished out of their sight) is known to be God. He is so recognized by Israel: "I have seen God face to face." This Man appeared to Abraham as "he sat in his tent door in the heat of the day." Abraham talks with Him. He and two with Him eat with Abraham; and they walk forth together and talk of the awful woe that waits over the cities on the plain below, and Abraham pleads with Him, and calls Him by a name. Long after He appears to Moses in the flaming acacia-bush in the desert, and Moses asks His name. The name is a strange one—"I Am." Again, Moses begs to see the face of Him who gave the law in the mount. God covers him with His hand in a cleft of the rock. He sees Him only as His glory passes by; "for there shall no man see My face, and live." And yet afterward, by the walls of beleaguered Jericho, Joshua sees a Man standing "with His sword drawn in His hand." And Joshua goes to Him. "Art Thou for us, or for our adversaries?" "Nay," is the answer; "but as

Captain of the host of the Lord am I now come. . . . Loose thy shoe from off thy foot; for the place whereon thou standest is holy"—just the warning to Moses before.

This Man, appearing, disappearing, speaking, warning, revealing, delivering, judging, is always recognized at last, worshiped, and called upon by a *name*.

No man can tell you the name. But wherever you find the word LORD in capital letters in our English version, that name stands in the Hebrew.

I say no man knows its sound. The Hebrew never uttered it. When he came to it he read another word, *Adonai*, which we translate "Lord." The other is the "incommunicable name"—the name especially peculiar and appropriate to the awful God. "No man hath seen God at any time; the only begotten Son, . . . He hath declared Him." "He that hath seen Me hath seen the Father." "All things were made by Him." The mystic, unutterable four Hebrew consonants, whose vowels are lost, which no man has ever spoken, spake the name of the Man who talked with Abraham, wrestled with Jacob, gave the law through Moses, drew His sword by the walls of Jericho. Mark now—for that is the point of the argument

—He is a Person. He has a name. It seems the main point of the teaching, the purpose of all those Old Testament revelations, was to make men understand that God is a Person.

There shall be no abstraction set before them to worship under vague sign and symbol; no Being or mere expression of power or of justice, much less of wrath and fury. There shall be a definite conception of the Power invisible, as One, and as a Man, whatever else He is, with a drawing toward men, and a possible, even loving, communion with men. He shall appear as a Man, and give His messages as a Man, and walk in the garden in the cool of the day; and yet the trailing glory of His departure shall proclaim the Bearer of the unknown name "of the mystic letters four."

Yet in the religion thus illuminated, taught, and impressed there shall be no similitude. I dare to say it is unexplainable by any thinkable law of development. Why did not the children carve an image of the Man their fathers believed to be God, and set it up as a memorial? In the places of His appearing it is the rude stone-heap, the cairn or cromlech, or the anointed pillar which marks the memorial. But "make no similitude; take heed to yourselves"—"no likeness of anything in heaven, or in earth, or in the water under the earth."

The Greek did it, and made his deities persons, but finite persons, with more power of hand and brain, but shameless of all passion and crime. The Egyptian believed in divine personality, and taught it in monstrous forms. The Hindu did the same, and in forms more monstrous and more bestial tried to realize the personality of the Powers spiritual.

One moves through these Egyptian, Assyrian, Hindu personalities divine as through a nightmare dream of hideous faces and bestial conceptions, in a madhouse universe.

The vague phantasms of the brain, Ormuzd or Ahriman; the formless, shapeless, shadowy Brahm of Eastern pantheism or Western dream; the Power that is no Power with any sense but what it finds in its own creatures—even these cloud-vanishing phantasms are a relief from the dog-headed, cat-headed, elephant-headed deities in which the nature-worshiper sought to express the personality of the invisible Powers.

Whence got the Hebrew Scriptures that bald and bold realism which personifies God as a Man, and yet never mistakes Him for a *mere* man? which gives Him human arms and hands and eyes and heart, a house, a throne, a footstool, a crown and a scepter, a sword and a bow, and yet sternly forbids any likeness, any image, any imagined resemblance?

They go farther. They give the awful Power unseen every intellectual and moral trait possessed by man. He is loving, He is angry; He is wrathful, He is pitiful; He swears, and stands by His oath; He repents, and changes His decree; He is utterly human, only without sin. There is no more intense, individualized, clear-cut personality in all history or drama than this God of the Old Testament, with the incommunicable name.

The utmost stretch of human genius in the creation of character has never yet approached the vivid individuality and personality of this Person, marked in those old books by the name forever hidden in the "mystic letters four."[1]

There is a wonderful thing extant for some years now, born in Germany—in whose theological schools Christ and His gospel are still on trial, as if Pilate's court were a perpetually sitting tribunal—and imported free from tariff or duty into England and America, called by somebody—for what reason I know not—"the Higher Criticism."

---

[1] יהוה

One might ask, If this be higher criticism, what *is* lower criticism, and what the *very lowest* at last?

Well, it is all pure guesswork, let me say at once, and in its most characteristic development may be understood from a learned book published in this country, called "The Shakespeare Cipher," by a very able man; and also by a new and better "Shakespeare Cipher," published by a learned doctor of medicine, to show that the whole mass of poetry we call Shakespeare's was written by Francis Bacon to abuse Queen Elizabeth, and send her down branded to all time, because she refused to acknowledge him, Francis Bacon, as her son by a secret marriage with his father when she was only the princess, the "Lady Elizabeth"!

In these two cases the Shakespearian critics know the language in which the book was written. It is their mother-tongue. It was written three centuries ago. In the other case there is not a man living who could pronounce a speech in Hebrew so as to be understood by Isaiah or Daniel (supposing there ever was an Isaiah or a Daniel!).

It is a sad thing to be idle, especially in a land where there are only books, pipes, and beer, and where a paternal government presides over a man's birth, education, religion, occupation, marriage, sickness, death, and finally his tombstone.

Turn him loose with the conception that all things—government, social order, politics, science, and the rest—are settled, untouchable even—indeed everything taken out of the arena of intelligent discussion except Christ and the Bible—and he must necessarily turn critic, and, if he has little to do, " higher critic."

The point I am desirous to emphasize is that this criticism, in the necessitudes of its conclusions, requires us to believe that a great many of the ideas, influences, and practices in the Old Testament came from Egypt, Chaldea, and Persia.

Of that, happily, you and I are just as able to judge as any critic; for it is not a thing of Hebrew consonants or masoretic vowels or accents, but of history and common sense.

Did the Hebrews, upon their return from captivity, reëdit or rewrite and reorder their sacred books under the influence of the Persian dualism? And do you so account for the final bitterness against all images, and the intensity of the monotheism thenceforward?

Well, I think you and I are quite competent to examine that, if we do not understand a word of

Hebrew. Ormuzd and Ahriman, the gods of eternal light and eternal dark, eternal good and eternal evil, are no more persons than the cloud that floats across the sky. They have not a single quality of personality. They are principles, whatever you may mean by that; names to express what the old Aryans believed they saw in life, time, the world, in the present and in the past; principles contending with each other, each now victor and now vanquished; but being Aryans, "children of light," having still retained enough of the old divine tradition to hold that men were on God's side and right's side and truth's side, and that the right would be master in the end, they stood by Ormuzd and exhorted men to do the same, and called their land Iran, "the land of light," and the Tartar world, the devil-serving world opposed to them, Turan, "the land of darkness."

They were our ancient cousins, and they believed in light, and taught their children to ride boldly, shoot straight, and tell the truth; and so let us honor their memory!

But from no notion of their vague principle Ormuzd can you derive the clear-cut, realistic Personality, the Man whose name is so awful that you may say God (El), or gods (Elohim), but you must not utter His, for one syllable of it spoken out would rend the heavens!

Are we afraid of anthropomorphism? It is a long word, and long words ought to scare unlearned people. You will find the word a terrible one, and a sect-brand and heresy name in church story.

But I want you to notice that neither Old Testament nor New is in the least degree disturbed by what the word means. It is, after all, only a Greek compound; and our new dictionary-makers are putting such—thousands of them—into our dictionaries of English, so that the biggest English dictionary of this year will be supplemented next year by a new one advertised to contain "one thousand new words not to be found in any other dictionary." These additional words are all Greek compounds—or slang; and the English dictionary "up to date" contains about five complete and distinct languages; and yet there is one entire English language—even two—which has never yet been put into any dictionary, and this to my personal knowledge![1]

---

[1] The negro dialect of the South and the negro dialect of the writers of Southern stories.

Now man was made in the *image of God.* That means (real, profound, spiritual theologians will tell you) in the image of the Son of God, the second Person of the Trinity—such a transcendent and overwhelming Personality that He has two natures: the infinite and awful nature of God, and the poor finite nature of man, each in its utmost fullness and perfection; and yet both these natures make but one Person!

That is the Nicene Creed upon Personality. That is the immensity of what our poor little Anglicized Latin word "person" means at its highest. Heaven help our human stuttering! but that is the best we can do. "Tell me, I pray Thee, Thy name." It could not be told then. It is only half understood now.

Years after, a man of Jacob's family—a greater and a better man—was riding through the same land, but on another errand. He was son of Jacob's best-beloved, of the tribe of Benjamin, and his name was Saul.

He was on his way to Damascus to arrest and drag forth men and women charged with the crime of worshiping, in the way men called heresy, the God of their fathers. He was to bring them bound to Jerusalem to be tried by the sanhedrim.

And on the road he too meets the Wrestler. The contrast is remarkable. Jacob was left alone; Saul was surrounded with armed men. Jacob's meeting was in the night; Saul's was in the high noontide. Jacob's Antagonist appears mysteriously and silently out of the dark; Saul's smites him to the earth with one burst of overpowering light, and calls him by his name.

But Jacob's question and Saul's are the same: "Who art Thou, Lord?" Jacob got no answer because he could not understand the name. It was ages too early. Saul gets his promptly: "I am Jesus whom thou persecutest."

Jacob was lamed by the touch of the awful Wrestler. Saul was blinded. Jacob went limping over Peniel; went limping all his life; bore the brand of the wrestle. Saul went with those poor scalded eyes of his—his "thorn in the flesh" —all his days, when the scales of total blindness fell from them, and pitifully begs consideration from the Galatians when he has no amanuensis like Luke or Mark or Timothy: "See with how large letters I have written unto you with mine own hand;" the straggling, clumsy, uncial letters —like a child writing "large hand."

But the answer—"Jesus whom thou persecutest." Now Jesus is just the Greek, Latin, and English form for the Hebrew Joshua—"He who saves," or "God who delivers," or "God's Deliverer." And *now* He can be understood in part.

The awful Wrestler with the souls of men in midnight loneliness of the desert, or in burning noon on the world's crowded highways, wrestles to save. Our God is the Deliverer. If He wrestle and lame, He wrestles to make a prince of God out of a knavish Jacob. If He wrestle and overthrow and blind the man stricken amid trampling horse-hoofs to the sand, He smites to *save*. His name is Joshua; and Saul rises smitten blind, as his great ancestor was smitten lame, but an apostle henceforth, a selected prince in the kingdom of heaven!

We are slowly coming to see that the spiritual law in the natural world is that there is no advance save by wrestle and pain, by bloody sweat and groaning agony. So men have developed. So the lowest forms of life have risen to the higher. So nations have builded themselves and become "the chosen people," to do the chosen work, the princely work of God!

But this law is an eternal law in the world

spiritual, and therefore its manifestation in the world we call natural.

The development of the man Jacob into Israel, the prince of God, is by anguish, sorrow, bitter pain—Gethsemane's blood-drops; the blinding on the road to Damascus, the laming on Peniel. Because there is no development of the pneuma but by these and the bitter cross, so there is no development of the psyche but by toil and suffering. Nay, no development of even the soma, the mere body, but by the same.

One might, if he had ears to hear, write, I think, the most wonderful poem on the sorrows of the material world, whose groans God must hear as it struggles upward. "The whole creation groaneth and travaileth in pain together until now."[1] The spiritual law is an awful law when set to work in the natural. I do not wonder we have pessimists.

But the law is not the expression of blind force. The birth-pains and writhing agonies of the regeneration of a world are not the tyrannous inflictions of brute power or blind machinery.

Behind all, over all, in all, rules and reigns the

[1] The victory and the redemption of the pneuma must precede the deliverance of the psyche and soma. The struggle of the natural must continue until the victory in the spiritual world, according to St. Paul.

Person, the Humanity, in whose image we are made, and whom we can understand.

Even *that* He declared of old in every vision of every seer. He came appearing in the likeness of the nature He was to take unto Himself forever in the mystery of the incarnation, consummated nineteen hundred years ago that December night under the Syrian stars.

He had His name in all the old story; an awful, mysterious name, declaring eternal existence and eternal power; but a name, a Person.

Taking on the reality of human nature and making that a part of the infinite Personality, He takes a name all men can utter, and all men understand; a name near and dear to souls blinded, staggering, struggling, hard-bestead; a name of victorious hope; a triumph cry to the muster, the march, the battle, and the victory, for a world groaning and travailing to the birth of the new day—"I am the Deliverer."

And He proved the name His own! Let us lay our earthly fancies down. We are Christian people. There are things on which our earthly philosophies babble—the best of them. The world is a world of onwardness; a world where every to-morrow is better than to-day; a world struggling up to the eternal daylight. That is our hope. It is more—it is our faith. We wrestle on. We will not let Him go till the blessing comes. And the faith weakens not, and the hope dims not, in all the sorrow of the burdened years, for we have now the name of the Man who is wrestling it into light. His name is JESUS; proved before our eyes in life and death. One far more than philosopher—though no philosopher greater—Sage and Seer of our own kindred, put our Christian thought in form for us all—the final proof to earthly sight of the name's truth. "I am Jesus," He cried, and

> " Those blessed feet
> Full eighteen hundred years ago
> Were nailed for our advantage
> On the bitter cross."

LECTURE III.

RESPONSIBILITY OF GOD.

I am the Lord, and there is none else, there is no God besides Me: I girded thee, though thou hast not known Me; that they may know from the rising of the sun, and from the west, that there is none besides Me. I am the Lord, and there is none else. I form the light, and create darkness: I make peace, and create evil: I the Lord do all these things. ISA. xlv. 5–7.

LECTURE III.

RESPONSIBILITY OF GOD.

GOD, as the books of the Bible represent Him, is One. That One is a Personality; but of such enormous personality that He is three Persons, and yet one God. There are those who stagger at this. I confess I cannot understand their mental condition. I am a poor little limited, finite existence; as far as anything I can see in this world, scarce a square inch in size or meaning. My poor little time is a few years between the eternal past and the eternal future; and a large number of those years are spent in unconsciousness, infancy, and childhood. A good share of the hours that are mine, when I really am conscious, are spent in unconsciousness. The night comes—an apparently arbitrary arrangement—and I am practically non-existent during many hours of the short period when I have some force of body and of mind.

And then comes the other dark again, and I am lost from all men's knowledge and memory as far as this life goes. Out of the dark, into the dark again. A few years between, of light and dark, of consciousness and unconsciousness, of doing and being tired of doing, the whirling spokes of light and dark spinning me on and away.

There are a few things I can do, millions of things I cannot do. Some few things I know or think I know; and if I am a writing or speaking man I try to write them or speak them, and succeed in some small measure. All the books ever written, all the speeches ever spoken, cannot contain the things I do *not* know; the things Plato and "broad-browed Verulam" did not know, much less the Parliament of Great Britain or the Congress of the United States!

I have seen great libraries—enormous provision of space for the collection of human knowledge. But you would be obliged to attach them all together—the Bodleian, the British Museum, the Bibliothèque Royale, the Astor, the Lenox, and, the grandest of them all for architectural dignity and spaciousness, the Public Library of Boston, and all the libraries of all the colleges in existence —to hold the books containing what the professors in all the colleges and universities in Europe and America do *not* know!

And yet, being only this, I have the dignity of personality! Am I to be startled, amazed, when I am told that the Power which makes, orders, and guides the universe is one God, and yet in that divine nature three personalities? If I were told there are a hundred or a thousand, I do not see why I should be at all staggered. When I apply my logic or my metaphysics to the infinite, I am as a beetle undertaking to lecture on astronomy. There is no common measure between the finite and the infinite. The infinite is not merely an infinite number of finites. Endless eternity is not an infinite number of days of twenty-four hours each.

There is but one possible point of touch between the finite and the infinite, and that point is ethical. There is no point common of power, of size, of extension, of force, of abidance, of knowledge. There is no point of comparison, no place or ground logical, where you can bring these two together, except the point of *moral obligation*.

And this moral obligation rests alone upon the fact of personality—no person, no obligation; no person, no responsibility. Mark it well, and it will save you from endless confusion.

There is no responsibility, no moral obligation in a cyclone; none whatever in a hurricane; none at all in the great sun over your heads; not the shadow of a moral responsibility in all the infinites and all the eternities.

Power behind phenomena expresses nothing but power if you leave it with that definition. As a being with moral responsibility, sense of duty and obligation, and conscience telling me "You must," I have a supreme contempt for all the infinites and all the unconditioneds, for sun, moon, stars, and all powers behind them; for I am far better than they, as the man is better than the brute. I have no reverence, and can get up none, and I certainly have not an atom of fear, for the power behind phenomena, unless that power can prove to me most unmistakably that it has sense, decency, some regard for right and truth, and, in fact, is using its faculties to do the best it can in its place.

Do not get scared, and do not abdicate your awful right of judgment in the face of mere brute force. It is man's prerogative to say, "This is right, this is wrong; this ought to be, this ought not to be;" and to say so at the mouth of a thousand bellowing cannon. And man has done it, and is doing it, and will keep straight on doing till he ends.

You cannot frighten us by your power behind phenomena, no matter how infinite and almighty that power is. I am a good deal better and bigger than that power, and pass judgment upon its performances, and praise or condemn them at my will, knowing that my judgments shall stand, and knowing that if the power behind phenomena is power only, I and my judgments shall still stand when phenomena and that sort of power behind them or in them have vanished into nothingness.

The power behind phenomena, to come into contact with men, must come as a person. There is that strange power in personalities that they can understand one another. And the essence of personality is moral responsibility. A person stands under obligation. It makes no difference whether he be a finite or an infinite person; he is under obligation; he is *bound* by law and duty.

Does it startle you to say that Almighty God is under obligation? Unless He is, you and I can have no spiritual relation with Him whatever; nay, not even an intelligent relation. We certainly can have no moral obligation toward any Being who has no moral obligation toward us. That is what makes the God of Calvinism, by His very definition, forever impossible. A Being whose sole motive of action is His own good pleasure is a Being with whom we have no common bonds. The only feeling would be one of abject, unreasoning terror. For the brave and the true it might some day be imperative duty to defy and resist Him in spite of the terror.

But the God who wrestles with man, and wrestles with him as a Man, reveals Himself as a Person, and as such in relations and under names of relation; and relations carry responsibility. The unrelated can have no responsibility.

He is a Maker, and a maker is responsible for what he makes. A man cannot make a wheelbarrow without assuming the responsibility of seeing that it will work, and that in working it will do no harm to anybody.

God reveals Himself as a King. It is another name of relation, of duty and responsibility. A king must govern his people. He must suffer with his people. He must keep watch and ward for his kingdom's safety. He must govern firmly, righteously, helpfully, mercifully. He is bound by webs of moral bonds to those over whom he rules, as they are bound to him.

God reveals Himself as a Father. Surely there is a name of obligation and responsibility here! A father—we all know a father's duties. And it is in such common household and familiar names that He tells men His character. A father must take care of his family; guard, shelter, feed, provide for, help his family, his children, his helpless ones.

Why are we afraid to take God at His word? Why shrink from the names He uses to reveal Himself? Why always fall back into the vagueness and inanity of our metaphysical irreverence—as if we thought God did not know Himself, and our spider-web words added somehow to His glory as Father and King?

Does He not know? Creator, King, Father, Householder, Shepherd, even Employer paying wages for a day's work—these are His chosen names; and these, you see, are all names of relation, and so of responsibility, obligation, and therefore of Personality.

Thus in a moral world we live moral beings, under a moral Lord and Government. The "Ought" rules over all, transcends all; reigns in the Personality of the Father and King.

It is an instinct with us to help the Almighty all we can. There is something in the fact that we are made in God's image that leads us, I suppose, to try to create even a universe, no matter how fantastically. And facing the fact of a world full of evil, pain, and sin, we want to explain it all in some way to save God responsibility.

Now observe He does not thank us! He has no wish to shirk any part of the responsibility. He has made the universe, and He stands by the consequences, and asks not the help of your metaphysics to argue Him out of His responsibility, nor your sentimentalities or theologies to apologize for Him!

The Persian dualism was a philosophy to account for the existence of evil, and yet hold to a good God. For myself, I confess that as a mere working hypothesis, apart from revelation, explanatory of facts as they are, it is the only hypothesis I as a reasonable man could admit. It is plain, direct, deals with the facts, and puts man on the side he, as a moral being, should occupy.

But—the Almighty, the Personality with the awful name, declines, by the mouth of the prophet, to be relieved of His obligations as Creator!

In the summons to " Cyrus, His anointed, whose right hand I have holden," the prophet proclaims the Personality, the unity, and the responsibility, in the face of Zerdusht and his two Principles: " I am the Lord, and there is none else, there is no

God besides me. *I form the light, and create darkness: I make peace, and create evil:* I the Lord do all these things." "Verily Thou art a God that hidest Thyself, O God of Israel, the Saviour."

It is only, I take it, the same desire to shield the Almighty from responsibility—a very amiable if a very weak and superfluous desire—which prompts some good people to hold such notions as restorationism—that is, that evil men and devils will find another chance somewhere, in some other world of trial, and be all "saved," as they call it, sometime; and still other good people to hold that all the unconverted will just pass into an eternal sleep, and only the righteous be immortal.

I have no quarrel with the temper of these dreams; but they make no appeal to my intelligence, and rather seem impertinent. The eternal Wrestler can take sufficient care of His own reputation; and if He declares Himself responsible for the evils of this world, and makes no excuse, responsible for the pain, misery, torment, and wretchedness of *this* world—I cannot doubt but He will justify Himself in any world, as He justifies His ways here, more and more, to human faith and human reasonableness. At all events, my poor, ignorant guesses are quite unnecessary, and perhaps, as apologies, impertinent.

The worship of a responsible God makes what some have called "the Scheme of Salvation" no "scheme" at all, but just the inevitable working of an inevitable law. As a "scheme" we know nothing about it. The Lord never revealed it as a logical scheme at all. He surely never taught men that "right views upon the Scheme of Salvation" were of any consequence.

The New Testament is just the blossom and fruit of the Old. God, being a responsible Father and King, must by inevitable law follow His own. The shepherd *must* go after the sheep which was lost. The father must meet the prodigal while he is yet far off. For the sheep is still the shepherd's; wheresoever it wanders, ownership is not changed. The son is still his father's son among the swine; not a whit less so than when the son wears the robe and the ring! Indeed, the title to wear the robe and sit at the feast was never forfeited at any time. It existed during all the swine-feeding; was promptly acknowledged the instant it was claimed!

For we are dealing with personalities. And personalities are permanent, and the relations between them are permanent also. Those connected with a personality that is infinite are infinite relations—from eternity to eternity.

So the revelation has been that of a suffering God. I take it for too shallow an opinion of the atonement to suppose it a three-years' life of poverty and a cruel death that men might have their sins forgiven in any judicial or commercial method, and by the misery and death of One have a happy and blissful Mohammed's heaven for all eternity! We cannot take Caiaphas's doctrine of atonement.

Surely there was larger and more rational purpose in the fact that the divine Wrestler with the souls of men took their own nature upon Him and became one of them, or rather, in His infinite humanity, *all of them*, and before their eyes wrestled with the world's sufferings, and suffered with its sore pains, and was bruised and wounded with its death, and died!

If suffering be the worst thing, could He choose it? If the ignominious cross and the long agony be essential evil, could He choose them and call on those He loved to take the same cross and follow Him? How strangely blind and half-heathenish do we still remain!

Is it not the revelation of a toiling, striving,

suffering God? Let us get rid of the phantom our poor philosophies impose upon us still, the best of us. We weave a God out of our own inner consciousness, and then attribute to Him the character we would have were we omnipotent, and omnipotent as He!

In days when king meant autocrat, men imagined Him an irresponsible despot, doing things solely for His own gratification. Even what we have dared to call Christian theologies have given Him a character and motives which, did they belong to a man, all free, honorable men would condemn with one voice of detestation.

It is not the character He gives Himself. He chooses His own name. He is bound to, and is responsible for, and suffers with His own creation. There is a depth of awful meaning in those words, "The Lamb slain from the foundation of the world." The tragedy of Calvary was an exhibition in time and space, that men might know forever of what goes on in the abysses of the divine nature out of time and out of space.

We Christians confess that Jesus of Nazareth was and is the Son of God. Now He had the power and also the wisdom—both, we profess, infinite—to choose whatsoever life, being the Son of

Man, that He would. He chose the life we all know. There was no constraint upon Him from without. But He had, we profess, a purpose. There was, then, the constraint of a purpose—a purpose formed within Himself out of the conditions of His own nature.

It was an utterly unselfish purpose. On that, not only all Christians, but all unbelievers who read His earthly life, are alike agreed. All our pulpits inform us that His life is the one model life for men. Would any of them dare to gainsay that statement? Would any pulpit anywhere, under the name of Christian, dare to assert that the life of Jesus of Nazareth was *not* the loftiest life conceivable for a man—the noblest, bravest, manliest, kingliest life?

We all agree with the pulpits. It is very strange, considering the way we ourselves want to live, but we all do!

But Jesus of Nazareth was God. He revealed God in His inmost character. "He that hath seen Me hath seen the Father." So, then, that life related in the Gospels is God's life. I do not want to escape the conclusion. If I did, I fail to see how I can; I am walled in.

Does it occur to us how utterly contradictory to

our common conceptions of the divine nature that life is? how utterly contradictory—as just a plain, bald "not so"—that life is to many of our accepted and most orthodox (so called) theologies?

I confess I am but a child feeling my way—most pitifully helpless and blind. The gospel is, to this day, a hidden mystery in most part. Those words and common works of Jesus of Nazareth are far more inscrutable mysteries to me than all the miracles of Old Testament or New.

I cannot "stand agaze at Joshua's moon in Ajalon" when I read that "after supper He took a towel, and girded Himself," and washed their feet; and that He who did so declared, "Have I been so long time with you, and yet hast thou not known Me, Philip? how sayest thou then, Show us the Father?" "I am among you as he that serveth." "Whosoever will be greatest among you, let him be your servant." Dare you follow out these things to the plainly suggested end? Will you turn, as your theologies and pulpits at once do, and begin to hedge?

I confess frankly my terror at what seems to be the only possible meaning. I dare not formulate it. I believe, however, that it is the very heart of the Catholic faith—a faith which looms larger and profounder as the years pass on; a faith as far beyond our complete understanding now as would have been the name Jesus to wrestling Jacob. But it is all there in that old Nicene Creed; and "the Church of the Future," of which we hear sometimes so much in very foolish talk, will just be a church large enough, holy enough, wise enough, to believe *all* there is in the Nicene Creed!

I just *dare*, and that only, to suggest it, and in a question: Does the Nicene Creed profess faith in a God who serves? Do the acts and words of our Lord Jesus Christ reveal a King who is the almighty and eternal and awful King—awfulest and highest—and who, because He is so, is the Servant of all? Did Jesus of Nazareth reveal not only a suffering God—we are all agreed on that, I suppose—but a responsible God, and therefore a *serving* God? "If I then, your Lord and Master, have washed your feet!" Think of it! If the highest place is the place of most obligation, of most service!

This is all with fear and trembling. But we are Nicene Christians here. We chant the faith of nineteen centuries; and it is a faith in Personalities and in facts concerning those Personalities. That creed rings round the world, on every land and sea. Its abysmal depths of living meaning will never be sounded till the stars are old. But I ask again: "Does not the Nicene Creed speak of a *serving* God?" Is not the one God, in the three Personalities, doing something all through—making and serving His worlds?

I say I am but a trembling and ignorant child, creeping, I trust not irreverently—certainly humbly—along the edge of vast abysses—the 'ορατα και 'αορατα—the visible and invisible depths and heights which I believe our Father has made and keeps. But I know He does nothing save by the eternal and immutable law of His own personality—and I know fathers *serve*. It is the load upon all of us who are fathers. Do we complain? Do we cast off the weak? Do we deny the disobedient? Do we not bear our burdens and make no sign? Do we not still hold to the relationship, and knit the broken knots, and try to keep the jeweled bond around the family complete? Well, "I believe in God *the Father Almighty.*"

But let us leave these heights and speak of men.

I say we are all agreed that the life of Jesus of Nazareth, which He declared revealed God—a thing neither the world nor the church can yet understand—is the divinely ideal life for men. The acceptance of that conclusion is the sole rational basis for the existence of this church; for our being here together; for our bishops, priests, deacons, and laymen; for our baptisms, confirmations, and communions.

Well, that certainly was a life of service! The mysterious Wrestler from the beginning with men stepped out visibly and revealed the law. "The invisible Powers wrestle with men; have done so from the beginning, will do so to the end. They wrestle to serve and to deliver."

How coolly we put it all by—"Tell me Thy name"! "Why askest thou after *My* name?" Do you not see we are in no case to understand it? Because we can only hear what our ears have the power to hear.

We understand Jesus, Saviour, in a small degree, and for that let us be thankful! "We are in misery, in stress, in pain, in sin, and wandering, turned out of our Father's house, lost sheep and lost children; and He has come to save us out of our trouble." That is a great deal! Our prayers, but especially our modern hymns, are full of that. We are grateful, or say we are, that Christ suffered, so that I may not suffer—grateful that He saves me from what I deserve. I still agree with Caiaphas that it is better another should suffer than that I should.

As it seems to me, that is about as far as we have ears to hear; as far as we can understand *the name*. But when we are asked to go on and accept the rest of the name—Saviour of all men—we do not understand; because our Lord came to reveal the *law* of salvation. For He was very plain about it: " He that saveth his life shall lose it: and he that loseth his life for My sake and the gospel's shall find it."

For, as I take it, our Lord put little weight on the question of pain. It must have been to Him a very small thing indeed. He deliberately chose it, you see. I think that "church of the future," when it comes, will get away beyond our present ideas about saving from sorrow, labor, or trouble, as the end of the salvation of Christ.

Our Father in heaven must be full of labor and sorrow, of care and pain and the bitter sense of loss. His eye is never closed in rest. His hand is over all His works. He grieves over the sins and wrongs of His world. He has a vast realm to administer, and He takes care that a sparrow, even, is not wronged. Infinite pain in the infinite heart of God!

Now our labor and care and anxiety in this world are all spent and exhausted, as a rule, on the effort to save ourselves from pain. That is about as far as we have yet attained. We are in that respect just where poor Jacob was at the ford of the little Syrian Jabbok!

Moralists write about this; preachers preach about it; satirists laugh at it. We are loading ourselves down, and making our lives bitter, narrow, comfortless, and slavish, to save ourselves from pain. The sight, thoroughly seen and appreciated, is pitiable. Beings supposed to have sense actually loading themselves, and groaning as they crawl under their loads, lest they should have to carry those loads!

One of the two or three most enormously and absurdly rich men in the country—dead now, and enjoying a little rest, I hope—said to me once, " I envy you." " Envy *me?*" I asked. " Yes; you are a free man, your own master, and doing and saying helpful things to people every day; and I am like a blind horse in a bark-mill, tramping the same monotonous path round the safe that contains the deeds and securities."

In the kindness of my heart I offered to relieve him at once of some part of his trouble, and bear his burden like a Christian brother, as St. Paul commands us.

I knew exactly where *five* millions would found a university to do enormous good and make his name a blessing forever; where another million would endow ten missionary bishoprics; where two millions more would build one creditable cathedral, and five millions another; and ten millions would be invested so as to relieve our Missionary Committee from the stress and anxiety they suffer; and then five millions more could be soundly invested so as to produce a respectable sum toward the instruction and Christianizing of our seven million negroes.

This would not have relieved him entirely—indeed, of only a fraction—of his load. He would still have been staggering under a burden which would crush *me*. You may be surprised, but it is nevertheless the fact, that he politely but peremptorily declined my kindly proposal, and groaned under it till the load crushed him, and left it, just as heavy, for his son to sweat under till he too is dead!

I sometimes think that nothing must so bring sorrow and pity to the sorrowful and pitiful heart of God as the sight of men like my friend, who load themselves down with such back-breaking and heart-crushing loads, and obstinately refuse help from heaven or earth!

And then the idiocy of it. For they are undergoing all this to escape a possible pain! They are toiling to escape toil! They are doing slaves' work to keep themselves free! And lo! the end comes, and their lives have had no more outcome and less enjoyment than the lives of their own grooms!

That God, with all His pity and tenderness, should worry Himself much over the labors and sorrows of millionaires is too much to expect, when there are so many ways open by which they can cease to be millionaires. "How hardly does a rich man enter into the kingdom of heaven!"

But the pain and toil of men to escape pain and toil are always tragical. And the conventional gospel that our Lord came to proclaim, as the greatest of all good news—that He was going to save them from all trouble by taking all trouble upon Himself—has not resulted yet in any great lessening of the sum of human anguish.

The conception of God as a Being supremely happy and supremely self-pleasing, who one day, out of the kindness of His heart, determined to take charge of some few, at least, of a wretched race, and save them all inconvenience and give them an eternal " good time," with nothing to do and everything to get, has become an unthinkable conception, I take it, to most thinking people. Nevertheless it is the conception, in some more or less modified form, which rules and commands acceptance in most pulpits, Protestant and Roman Catholic.

Suppose we rise to the other conception—that this world is a world of stress and strain, of bitter sorrow and stinging pain, of heavy, groaning loads, of aching hearts and broken backs; that our Father made it so because, being the world He wanted in His wisdom and for His purposes, He must make it so by the necessities of His purpose.

Suppose its pains are " growing-pains." It must be wrestled with to get it up to princedom. The wrestle is long. The night is long—ages long, as men count ages! And in the wrestle the awful Wrestler Himself touches and *lames*.

But the Maker of the world is responsible for His world! He too has no " happy time " with it, I think. He too is wrestling the long night through. And to teach men that " happiness is " *not* " our being's end and aim," He reveals His own character by actually coming to live this life.

Not to shun pain in it, but cheerfully, freely, gladly to accept it *as the law*. " Our being's end and aim " is to get up, to climb higher, to ascend, by any path, no matter how toilsome. Our salvation is not deliverance from pain, but deliverance from halfness, low-downness. Our salvation is to be *raised*. " If I be lifted up, I will draw all men unto Me." He *was* " lifted up," but upon a cross!

Let us disabuse our minds of pagan ideas. Our God does not "lie beside His nectar, careless of mankind," like the gods of Greek Olympus. As to the gods of German metaphysics, I personally know nothing; nor does any living man—or dead one either, for that matter. The only God I know, the only God that any sane man can know, I think, is Jesus, who was born in Bethlehem, and was in stress and strain all His earthly life!

He is a wrestling God. He does not seem to have cared to be " happy." He does not seem to have thought that idleness, wealth, freedom from care, rich food, fine houses, fine clothing, the regard or reverence of men, were at all desirable or necessary. Let us not destroy the force of this, and lose the gospel, by the poor theological conclusion that He lived this sort of life as an exceptional, temporary thing for a few days, all the time anxious to have it over and get out of it, so that He could have a happy time again!

Can eternal God live a temporary life? Can He play a character in a stage-play? Pardon me. But we must be reverent; we must be honest. "Jesus Christ the same yesterday, to-day, and forever"—there is no dramatic exhibition for a few years suggested *there!*

I am not concerned to "reconcile" all this with the imaginations of the metaphysicians. I have only to call your attention to the fact that God reveals Himself as a wrestling God from Genesis to Revelation.

There is even a suggestion that He is worn with the strain: "Let Me go, for the day breaketh."

But He owes a blessing, and acknowledges the debt and the power of the sorely tried and lamed world upon Him: "I will not let Thee go, except Thou bless me." A wrestling God in a wrestling world!

And so I think we have the meaning of the world and our own. We are poor and very far down yet. One is tempted to use the almost threadbare words of our "working hypothesis" development here. They will fit in very well, if you will try the experiment, with the soundest Nicene orthodoxy.

We can surely not dream that any of us are living Christian lives—I mean by the measure our Lord revealed. Our comfortable lives, or our lives which we are straining all our faculties to make comfortable—it is all the same—are these Christ-like? Surely we are semi-developed Christians!

Take any of our congregations on a Sunday morning, from bishop or rector through all the pews. How many have the most shadowy likeness to the idea of Christ? Is not the idea of every man and woman—I will not say of every child, for "of such is the kingdom of heaven"—that the important business for which they are put into the world is to make themselves comfortable, and shun, as far as possible, all trouble and all pain? And if they are especially pious and devout, will they not plead with God to help them do this?

I am not speaking of mere respectable animal men, nor of the pitiable and pitiful women whose personality and responsibility begin and end with what is called "Society"; I am speaking of men with ideas, and of women who have brains under their bonnets, and good hearts under the revers of their jackets, and some true faith in God and duty. Is not the idea this: that the religion of Christ is meant to comfort and help them out of or under any trouble or pain they may have; that they are right to try to have as little as possible; and that God, who has infinite hoards of happiness which He does not need, ought to be worshiped and prayed to for the sufficient supply they need in sickness, sorrow, loss, or death?

Now consider. Jesus Christ was not the exceptional Man. It is you and I that are exceptional. We are the oddities, He is normal. He consequently reveals law; and, being God and Man in one Person, He reveals eternal law—that is, the law of God's nature, which is the law for this world, and for every possible and conceivable world.

And that law clearly revealed is that comfort is not the highest aim here or anywhere for a man, nor for a divine Man; that salvation is not deliverance from pain here nor anywhere; that salvation is victory—by no matter what toil and bitterness endured; that man, God's child, made in the image of God, is not a pain-fearing being, but a wrestling and a conquering being; that his business is to get up—to become a prince, to have power with God and men, and to prevail, though he may be lamed, crippled, in the process; that the strain, wrestle, laboring of congested lungs and panting muscles are nothing if so be that he "prevail"; that God wrestles also like a man till the breaking of the splendid dawn!

So you have the law of human life, which is the law of the universe, revealed—the law of responsibility!

When we make a final settlement of social questions which we are dilettantizing over now, it will be on the basis of that law. It may be a long time in coming, but it is bound to come in the end. We may have many upheavals and many even bloody revolutions, for what I know, before the end comes. But the end will come from no evolution —though some may think so—of any principles of its own, much less of any bread-and-butter and animal-comfort principle of our socialists.

Let me state it: responsibility is destructive of what people call comfort. The more intense the sense of responsibility, the less "comfort." The only beings comfortable, "happy," in the sense of our political economists, are animals or the lowest races, or the lowest among the higher races. When all sense of responsibility, of moral obligation, is gone, moral and spiritual pain is gone.

To be "perfectly happy"—in the sense of these people, that is—one must get rid of all conscience of responsibility. But what then remains? The happiness of a swine. The higher men go, the intenser their sense of personality—that is, responsibility, obligation, and duty—the more full of care, anxiety, and pain they are, the more unhappy.

To use the word of Mr. Herbert Spencer and carry his thought higher, the more "differentiated" any being is, the more exposed it is to pain and unhappiness. The highest conceivable being is exposed to the highest conceivable pain.

But the pain with us results from growing. No pain, no rising. "No cross, no crown!" How often we have seen those words put up in church decorations or in "floral decorations," without the slightest notion of their profound meaning!

The eternal Man was "lifted up" to draw the generations after Him, but lifted on a cross. No man can be "lifted up" otherwise; no people can be, no people ever has been.

The loftiest men since the beginning, the men crowned and sceptered, have been the men who cheerfully, but from afar, took sorrow, pain, and labor on them, and trod the footsteps of the Man of Galilee. "For the salvation of their souls?"

Oh, surely, if you know what the salvation of a man's soul means. But I do not think they much thought of that. Their prime idea was the Lord's. They were trying to save other men; trying to help up and on the lame, the weary, and the hopeless. They had—and did not know it nor care about it—read the riddle of the universe—that climbing means weariness; that the attainment of the upper heights means pain; that royalty is service; that the Creator and the Father has a universe to remake and regenerate on His hands, ("develop," if you will; there is nothing paralyzing in a word), and has a sore struggle doing it; and that those who are called His sons accept the law—the higher, the more bitter the winds blow, the colder the long snow-summits; but the sunlit splendor of the dawn must be reached, not for rest or enjoyment, but because they are "lifted up," nearer service and nearer God, though the soul goes limping over Peniel!

LECTURE IV.

RESPONSIBILITY OF MAN.

I am not alone, because the Father is with Me.
JOHN xvi. 32.

LECTURE IV.

RESPONSIBILITY OF MAN.

SOME time ago we had in our newest city—the newest city in the world, indeed—a thing called a fair—the Columbian Fair.

Among the attractions to draw people and their half-dollars to this fair there was, besides "the Midway Plaisance," with its alleged Turkish dancing-women and its alleged Hindu nautch-girls, a show called the "World's Parliament of Religions."

All the "religions" in the world were invited most politely to come there and display themselves and say their best say, and tell how they came to be "religions" at all.

Hindu yogis, Mohammedan dervishes, Roman Catholic cardinals, Buddhist bonzes from China, and "mahatmas" (whatever they are) from Arabia were invited to disport themselves side by side with Presbyterian and Unitarian doctors of divinity, with Mormon elders and archbishops of the Orient, and show a waiting and eager world which religion of all had the most to say for itself, and was, on the whole, the most picturesque and pretty specimen of "religion" now existent.

Altogether it was the most astonishing sideshow of a remarkable fair, and could have been imagined and attempted only in the freshest and youngest community on earth—a community which has not yet quite found out what itself means, is dimly groping, mostly on all-fours, toward a somewhat indistinct conclusion, but which, by its very existence, as the gathering-place of all men—a sort of *colluvies gentium*—has not settled the question of any divine purpose and meaning in itself, much less in the world; and yet, nevertheless, has a divine purpose and meaning, which in due time, and perhaps after much misery and many stripes, will appear.

Well, the fair was held, and the parliament was held, with results. The outcome of it all has not yet been published to a waiting world. Roman cardinals remain Roman cardinals still, and Hindu yogis are just as ragged and smell just as strong as ever, and the entire generation of cranks remain cranks still, and seem to be continuing their species numerously.

But the story had gone abroad into all lands that "the West" is rich. Indeed, it is a superstition even in Europe that all Americans are millionaires. I wish we were—at least that bishops were! How our missionary work would drive forward were that the case!

So the hungry children of the East came swarming with all their rags and all the populations and odors thereof—came swarming to the "Streets of Cairo" and the "Convent of La Rabida," and all the other shows—Chinamen, Javanese, Spanish monks, Buddhists and Brahmans from Hindustan, picturesque and ragged Syrians from Jerusalem, and venerable rabbis from Poland arm in arm with still more long-bearded and unkempt muftis from everywhere *except* Constantinople!

They came for those new Columbian fifty-cent pieces, and to exhibit incidentally their "religion." Nowhere but in the wildest dream could such an exhibition be taken as serious.

Of course it was not serious to the gentle, low-voiced children of the East. They were after the spoils of the West, and many of them were left—

as they no doubt were willing to be—stranded upon our hospitable and happy shores.

Many of us have no doubt had experience of these picturesque waifs and strays of the great fair—the *flotsam* and *jetsam* of the famous "Parliament of Religions"—at our back doors begging for cold victuals and old clothes, and without a solitary grain of profound Eastern psychology or any practical doctrine of reincarnation, an ounce of "theosophy" or a spark of "astral spirit," concealed about their fragrant persons!

One of the fragments of this drift, whose melodious name I have several times seen in print, professed to be a monk of some sort—Brahman or Buddhist, I know not which; but for the present a peculiar kind of monk, emancipated from all rules that usually govern monks. There are such "dispensations," I understand, among all sorts of monks. He could eat with anybody who gave him anything nice to eat, and drink anything nice that was going, and live in general intercourse with us benighted Christians, and take no harm, because his ecclesiastical superior in India had dispensed him from his vows for this time and occasion only; or else because—which sometimes occurs—being an "order" of monkery all by himself, and therefore his own "superior," he had just dispensed himself!

He was very picturesque. I do not, I say, know whether he was Brahman or Buddhist or Mohammedan, though I think certainly not the last. But it is of no consequence. He was a monk of some sort, and wore a long woolen skirt down to his heels and a roll of yellow stuff on his head, and people were interested in him on that account to start with. (A man's "environment" may sometimes have great influence on other people and very little upon himself.)

Women especially were interested in him. Women always are profoundly interested in monks. I think they always will be. There is here a psychological question more subtle and more interesting than any like question in Buddhism or Brahmanism. It deserves a book all by itself by some wise and learned man, so *I* leave it.

One lady—cultivated, thoughtful, an American woman of the best type—told me how much she was impressed by this mild-eyed son of the Punjab, and how devoted and pious and spiritual-minded he seemed to be.

She told me how he admired the enormous energy and victorious march of this Western civilization. To be sure, our religion was nothing—a thing of yesterday. It could have no influence on the mind—the gigantic mind—of the Hindu trained and fed on theosophy and reincarnations, and guided generally by "mahatmas" and astral spirits—the lofty and spiritual-minded Hindu, who adored Siva and Kâlî and Juggernaut, and who was quite content to be a slave, and make slave's slaves of his women. But we were far before the Hindu in some things—our machinery, our steam-engines, our electric dynamos, and the like.

Then he was staying here in the United States, and hoping to get help to establish an Industrial School—a School of Mechanics and Engineering, of McCormick's Reapers and Singer's Sewing-machines, of Patent Plows and Remington Typewriters—for his poor countrymen. In these and such as these, according to him, lay the future hope of the millions of Hindustan. Here was where they acknowledged our superiority. (I think he did *not* mention Pears', or indeed any kind of *soap*.)

Not at all in Bibles (modern thing, your Bible!), not in creed or prayers (a poor thing of yesterday, your creed and prayers!—read the hymns to Agni and Varuna), but in steam-engines, electric motors, in trolley-cars and the like, lay the redemption of Hindustan, as far as we uninspired Westerns could redeem it. In return for these they would send us some " mahatmas "; and there is as yet no tariff on " mahatmas."

I reminded my friend *first* that of all human creatures alive the Hindu is the biggest liar (the Syrian always excepted); that he really cannot speak truth save by accident; that all writers who know our Hindu cousins testify with one voice to this, even down to Mr. R. Kipling; and that the higher his caste and the more religious the Hindu is, the more measureless liar he is!

Of course I would not venture to say that this gentleman, who had come all the way to our barbarous country, and had run the risk of deadly defilement and the spoiling of his Brahm by being among us, was deliberately deceiving; but it was nevertheless the fact that the British government had established universities and colleges and schools of the very kind he named, and was trying to establish more among his people; and one of the greatest difficulties—indeed, the most serious of all—was their absurd, wicked, and inhuman system of caste, which stood in the way, and their ridiculous religion, which barred the road against all human investigation,[1] and tied a man helpless in the dirt-universe, which was mightier than he, and which he dare not investigate. Suppose his reaper should cut off a cobra's head! Suppose his locomotive should run down a cow! The consequences are awful, considering the religion which makes cobra and cow alike an incarnation of Brahm.

"But," I said, "here is what ought to be said, with all strong, honest utterance, to a soul drowned in worm-eaten shams and conceit like this poor man; to a soul for whom Christ died, steeped and stupid in hereditary lies:

"'Your people are, all things considered, the most abject people on earth. We have your vaunted "sacred books," and can read them as well as you. There is absolutely nothing in them! Your hymns to Agni (*Ignis*), the fire you cook your rice on, your chants to Varuna (οὐρανός, the sky and clouds), are the cleanest of your litanies. There are others of your sacred books—your real, practical sacred books of your practical religion (Sivaïsm, Saktaïsm)—of unutterable vileness, "their manners none, their customs beastly;" and your religious shows and processions, your temples and their ornaments, and the

[1] See "Code of Manu," *passim.*

sacred chariots and thrones of your idols are unimaginable for their foulness by any soul in this country; and yet you exhibit all these vile things as holy before the eyes of your children. Your sacred rites corrupted ancient Rome to infamy. They would have corrupted modern England but for the stalwart faith in the Lord Christ which declared your gods to be devils![1]

"'For all the historic period you have been slaves. Your own native rulers have been monsters of brutality, bloodthirstiness, and obscenity. Only under some foreign conqueror, from Alexander down, have you had a glimpse of justice, of order, or of settled rule—a slight suggestion that the world was not managed by beasts.

"'Your "religion," as you call the consecrated imbecility and foulness which has dominated your unhappy souls and bodies, has chained you down victims to any human animal strong enough to lord it over you. When he has proved himself strong enough, you have gone on all-fours and licked his feet.

---

[1] I need scarcely say that the religion of Hindustan has not been Vedic for centuries. The Vedas, the Brahmanas (sacrificial and priestly forms) are childish. The sacred books of the practical religion (which is the foulest idolatry) are worthy of the religion of Siva and Kâlî.

"'In one of the fairest and fruitfulest lands on earth you have lived in the mire for ages.

"'The only monuments of your labor are the temples of your brutal gods and the palaces of your almost as brutal rajas, whom nevertheless you have considered divine.

"'You have starved in your wretchedness and rotted in your cholera. You have let the beasts destroy you and the serpents poison you. You have had no energy, no manliness, and no hope.

"'There are two hundred millions of you, and two hundred thousand Englishmen govern you; and for the first time in all your recorded history they have given you a decent, orderly, just government, so that a ryot's rice-field is securely his own, his mud hut and his wife and children belong to himself, and you are no more allowed to burn women alive as a holy obligation.

"'And you, and such as you—the Brahmans and the sacred men, the monks and holy men—are, in all ways you can, putting obstacles in the way; taking advantage of the educational opportunities given you by Christians, and then sneering at the hand that gives them and at the principles which are trying to save your wretched people into something human; in your hereditary conceit and imbecile slavery to the idea of your own superiority —what you call, poor creatures! your "divinity"—doing your utmost against the detestable Christian and revolutionary principle which declares a Pariah just as good as a lazy Brahman with his holy string!

"'No! It is not machinery you want, but Christianity. Strange as it may seem to you, that is nevertheless the practical fact. For mind, Christianity is in no sense a religion, as you Orientals take religion. It is not a means of getting a man out of trouble and toil and heartbreak. It is rather an arrangement which puts him into these neck-deep. The things you call religion have for their end the saving men from labor, pain, and struggle. This strange religion of the West—this religion of the Man who worked in the carpenter's shop at Nazareth—calls them to all three; proclaims all three blessed, human, and divine; proclaims them victorious, royal, masterful over a universe governed by reason, as we believe it— not by brute force, as you believe.'"

For the religions of the East all have the same dread of personality. To be rid of this burden is to be blessed. To drop into the infinite life of the impersonal, as a snowflake drops in the ocean;

all, to float as the same drop vaporized floats into the fleecy cloud-flocks of even and disappears in the splendors of the sunset; to cease to be personally conscious; to be rid of pain and toil, rid of all duty and responsibility, and dissolve into the infinite azure deeps—this is attained beatification, this is Nirvana and everlasting bliss!

To cease to have anything to do, anything to say; to be rid of responsibility, which means to be rid of personality—the words are equivalent—makes this heaven of imbecility man's highest hope, and you have destroyed all we Western races call manliness, courage, energy, and whatsoever else is high and noble. The world is too much for humanity. It becomes its master. Man stolidly accepts slavery, disease, hunger, the poisonous reptile, the jungle, man-eating tiger. He crouches helpless before any brutal thing in nature or in man. He submits, not nobly protesting, like a knight smitten down in the strife, fighting to the last gasp; but like a whipped cur who can only crouch and moan and sneak and whine for pity from a savage master!

There is no conquest of the world in *him*, no mastering of nature possible. He deifies the cruel powers that destroy him, and carves monstrous images of obscene and bloody things, and worships the bestial and the foul; for the bestial and the foul seem strongest, and there is no call from the divine to resist. He digs out his caves of Elephantis, puts his monstrous gods there, and flees the sunlight and the green earth.

Meanwhile the unbroken jungles shelter the venomous cobra and the tiger, and keep safe the seed-beds of the pestilence. He pollutes with filth the waters of his sacred river, and lays out his dying by its side, while the corpses are whirled away on the yellow wave, shadowed by the overhanging obscene birds that batten on the ghastly forms. For the river is too much for him. He has not thought of restraining it. It overwhelms his fields, and sweeps his mud hovel and his little harvests of rice away; so he calls it sacred, and worships Gunga as a god! The man of the Christian West comes, "levees" Gunga as he levees the Mississippi, and still the Hindu believes, for the present, that Gunga is a god! Brahm is far away, impersonal, and also helpless. Some day the Hindu will be lost to toil and sorrow, name and fame, in the immensity of Brahm—absorbed; a personality no more.

Conceive a people whose religion, so called, is

based upon the idea that existence is the sorest curse; that personality is punishment and the heaviest penalty; that to cease to be is the supreme good! Will such a people invent, improve, advance, conquer? There comes now and then to the surface a sign that here and there among ourselves there exist people who can talk and even write sentimentalisms about things they do not understand, and feign to exploit "the Oriental religions." They affect even to sneer at missions and missionaries, and admire bonzes, and talk about mahatmas.

Now we know India pretty well. She has not been hidden from the world's eye all these centuries. We know what her religions have done for her—where they have left her people—and we can make up our judgments upon what strong, just, righteous, and somewhat Christian rule has done for a people abject—made so inevitably by their "religion"!

It is the preëminence of Christ's religion that it emphasizes and demands the name of the person: "What is thy name?" It calls out the "I" to face the situation. No teacher was ever so aggressively personal as Jesus. He preaches continually His own personality. He cries, "Come unto *Me;*" "*I* will give you rest;" "Take *My* yoke upon you;" "*I* am the good shepherd;" "*I* am the door;" "*I* am the true vine;" "*I* am the way, the truth, and the life;" "No man cometh unto the Father but by *Me.*" It is because we have heard it all so often, I suppose; because it has become a part of our unconscious thinking, that we are not startled by the strangeness of this persistent and matter-of-fact preaching of Himself.

There is this peculiarity, also, about His dealings with men about Him, that He calls out the personality of all who approach Him. In some cases it seems as if the miracle were impossible till the personality assert itself. It is *will* on His part: "Lord, if Thou *wilt*, Thou canst make me clean." It is faith on the suppliant's part: "If thou canst *believe*, all things are possible to *him who believeth.*" The conscious assertion of the selfhood, of the individuality, is called for—the two persons must recognize each other, and face each other, and know each other by name before there can be effect.

Is not the act of faith itself a supreme realization of a man's own individuality, and a strong grasp upon the individuality of the Deliverer? "I will not let Thee go, except Thou bless me."

"Who gave you this name?"—the Catechism is true to the religion of personality. "A white stone, and in the stone a new name written," "the names written in the Lamb's book of life"—are not these things all on the same line?

Is not personality sacred because God is infinite Personality? And because man is made in the image of God, and therefore a person, is not his personality sacred in the eyes of God?

For mark, God never overrides the personality of man. He persuades, He leads in wise—infinitely wise—ways, and the convincing Spirit whispers in the heart, and Jesus stands forever at the door and knocks; but the independence of the personality is never outraged. A man shall be delivered by his own choice. He shall climb to the princedoms of God, but he shall be the "I" and say the "I" at every step.[1]

With a wonderful care the Eternal Personality treats the finite. No angel overrides the poor human will, nor breaks into the sacred circle of a man's individuality. Only devils from the outer chaos do that, and are cast out when the Lord of persons speaks the word of power to guard His own.

---

[1] In nothing does Calvinism more outrage Christianity than in its doctrine of "invincible grace."

One word here. Are we always reverent to the personality ourselves? Do not well-meaning people who go to help in warm brotherly kindness often trample rudely and thoughtlessly upon the feelings—that is, the individuality—of the poor or the suffering they would aid? Do they consider always the reserves and reticences of the heart to which a soul *with a name* is entitled? Do not we sometimes brusquely, and in unmannerly fashion, break into the sacred solitary rooms in which the soul sits alone—or at least try to? Remember Jesus " stands at the door, and knocks." He will never enter till the door is opened. If you would have Him guest you must invite Him.

Children are often wronged grievously by most loving parents. They have a right to themselves. Their personality is sacred. They have a right to their childish reticences and the little hedge that protects their individuality. It is frightful to hear such an expression as " breaking a child's will." God breaks no man's will. He seeks to make the will right. Let us older folk be careful about offending " one of these little ones," who are persons in the image of Christ, and have names by which He calls them, while their angels do always behold the face of the Father.

There is a terrible loneliness in personality. The soul bears its heaviest loads alone. It enjoys its profoundest blessedness alone. It suffers alone, it repents alone, and it leaves the world alone. Friends may be very dear and very desirous to aid or sympathize. "The heart knoweth his own bitterness." One must wrestle alone. There are times when the nearest and dearest—our heart's best brother—can only stand without. Kind hands may be eager to clasp ours, and loving lips desire to comfort, and ready feet to follow us to the brink; but each of us must step down into the dark, cold water *alone.*

I take it, in its real sense, no man ever heard a genuine confession. There are chambers in the soul into which no human foot can enter—of dearest friend or holiest priest.

For in the extremest assertion of personality there can be but one Companion. In the night-wrestle the antagonist is Jesus. In His own wrestle to come He tells His friends, "The hour cometh, yea, is now come, that ye shall be scattered, every man to his own, and shall leave Me alone: and yet I am not alone, because the Father is with Me." In the vast halls of loneliness the only sound is the echo of the footsteps of God!

The human personality and the divine have alliance. "If I ascend up into heaven, Thou art there: if I make my bed in hell, behold Thou art there" also. The human has something of the awfulness of the divine.

It is a trust, this personality, and a trust to make one tremble; for as far as we know, it is never recalled. A man can never get away from his past. "The dead past," in the pitiless strength of human personality, is not dead and has no dead to bury.

A man's words and works are stamped with his own individuality, branded with his brand, and marked with his own signet. He cannot make the word unspoken, nor the deed undone. He puts something of his personality into all he does, and there back of him they lie, the creations of his own will gone out into the yesterdays, but living still.

Even Almighty God—I say it reverently—cannot destroy a fact, cannot make that undone which has been done. He can forgive the sin—"cut off the entail of sin," as Jeremy Taylor speaks; but He cannot make the sin not to have been committed. So a man projects himself and stamps himself upon the universe. It is a compelled scientific conclusion that the words we say here will still exist in the material earth while it shall stand. We are changing the relations of the atoms about us every word we speak, and that changes the relation of others; these are, of course, mingled with other changes and to ears are lost; but we know that we hear but a small fraction of the sounds about us, and it is quite conceivable, as a purely scientific matter, that there may be ears which hear all the noises, and the shouts and chargings, the volleying repulse, the thunder of the cannon, and the saber-clash of the last charge at Waterloo.

It is curious that they are not the incidents of yesterday which age brooding by the fireside remembers best, but the incidents of childhood, the friends long dead, the acts and words gone into the past; and more than curious—suggestive of things terrible—that some boyish escapade, some little mean thing done, which had no special consequences, comes back more vividly to torment the conscience than some large wrong of manhood!

It has a terrible side to it, this personal life. It makes all things so frightfully, uncompromisingly real. "I did this; I said that. I have issued the coin from the mint of my personality. I cannot recall. I have created something. God help me if it be evil! The Lord deliver me from myself!"

But this stern, masterful religion of the Lord Christ leaves us no escape from the awfulness of the gift, nor from its terrible responsibilities. Instead it tells us to thank God for it; to strive more and more for its larger measure; that our blessedness comes from the intensity and aggressiveness of our personality; that it is a growth into the likeness of eternal God to become more and more a person, an "I," with every personal trait and quality alive—will, affection, faith, love, hope; that the word "I will arise" is forever the word of power that delivers when the lost child goes home.

And now upon the world and men see the effect. There is but one companionship eternal for the human person—namely, the divine Person. So sure is this that the divine Person took human nature—that is, all human personality—into one Person, never to be divided!

Man walks with God. God encourages him to walk like God; shows him his responsibilities as a person in a world made and ruled by a Person; shows him his obligations and moral responsibilities, and urges him up and on.

Well, in some faint and half-hearted way the Christian peoples have seen this, and are trying to fulfil their obligations in the high place God has given them. Christianity, because it is a personal religion, is aggressive. It means will. It counts strength good; not as such only—it has small regard for dumb or irrational force. Christ *ordered* the tempest to close its bluster, remember. The highest force, the force to be reverenced because it is ordered, rational, and spiritual, the force to be obeyed, is the force of a personal will. Power displaying itself as power is not on God's nor man's side. It is diabolic, rather. Power that speaks conscience, orderly will, help and not harm, salvation, not destruction, is the power our faith holds divine.

I have heard wonder expressed that the religion of the mild, pitiful, and gentle Jesus should be the religion of the warrior peoples, the aggressive, conquering peoples of the world. One may remember a book published some years ago by a very interesting man, who tried to construct a new religion from Brahmanism and Christianity. The book was called "The Oriental Christ." The object was to show that the mild Hindu is repelled by our aggressive, masterful Western Christ, and that to convert the Hindus we need to present only the tender and pitiful Christ.

Possibly some of us thought there was more of sentimentalism than of religion in this. Yet the writer was clearly honest and sincere; and there are those among ourselves who have been slow to see that the Lion of the tribe of Judah, the Captain of the Lord's host, and "the King of kings, and Lord of lords," with His "vesture dipped in blood," is none other than the Nazarene—the Lamb slain from of old.

But why should it surprise us that a religion which teaches that the building up of personality is the aim of living, life, and effort for man; that onward and upward toward the highest is the path marked for him; that the infinite Person in whose image he was made calls him to imitate Himself—why should it surprise us, I say, that such a religion should train the leaders and masters of men?

To believe that there is an eternal relationship between myself and Almighty God; that such is the relationship that when none else can come near me He is with me; that though there were not another being in the universe but myself, He would be with me; that this relation, *personal*

—between persons, not abstractions nor ideas—shall stand

> " When the stars are old,
> And the sun grows cold ; "

that I am here in His world to help Him do His work in it in masterful and royal fashion; not to shun toil, but to court it; not to shirk responsibility, but to bear it; not to enjoy, but to suffer, as needs must suffer every creature who will climb higher, every man and race of men who are wrestling out of the old dark into the new dawn; and that, if so be, I must wrestle with eternal God Himself alone, that the old cowardice may perish and the new courage may be born, and so I emerge a prince, at last prevailing, though I go limping on the heights of Peniel—this belief, even part grasped and part lived poorly, will give you the men who are victorious.

Believed so as to be lived, and fear is gone; fear of all power save the power ordered, moral, righteous, takes departure. A man himself says, yet with no arrogance and no insolence—with profound reverence, rather, and a noble humility—" I am a *person* here among *things*. I have reason, judgment, and a sense of righteousness; I am an 'I,' and deliberately make my resolution: 'I will arise.' Being what I am, I am *bound;* I am under obligation to all around me; I *must* stand for the best. The worst is my enemy. There are endless days before me; I cannot rest. 'My Father worketh hitherto, and I work,' said the one Son of God, in whom and by whom I too am a son; and I am called to work till the hour strikes."

There is all the onwardness, you see, all the restless energy, all the high hopefulness, all the dauntless courage of the leaders and the lords who have felled the forests, cleared the jungles, drained the marshes, and made the homes and the cities of men; have gone one long stride higher and made ordered governments, rights, and justice for men; and another stride higher still—have built churches and vast cathedrals, hospitals and homes for the outcasts of a yet semi-barbarous civilization, proclaiming that men have a Father in heaven, and that the most wretched one of all the family is still a person, and has relations with the rest, and especial relations with the Person who is from everlasting to everlasting!

Nirvana for him! Nay; neither here nor anywhere, neither now nor forever! In the vast worlds and æons the "I" can have no rest. It has been branded by the awful brand of the eternal " I," and branded for everlasting. Evermore across the ford that divides from home and Father's house he must go limping. He must stagger on over the heights of Peniel!

In a universe where all things change the person stands permanent. No slow wearing of the years, no chance nor change, no sudden shock of force, no earthquake, no cyclone, changes the person. The " I " stands self-conscious in all the years. It stands apart and looks at all else from the point of its own poise.

It will watch a star die out in the ethereal deeps, (a sun that is, and a system, and whatsoever these hold), and think its thoughts and write out its speculations in the calmness of a fixed assurance that, come what will to suns and stars and systems, *it* will stand outside and still say, "*I* think," and, "*My* opinion is thus and so."

It is impossible for the developed personality to imagine the universe existing and he not there! It is impossible for it to imagine a universe destroyed and he not there to see!

So our religion gives us no respite. We cannot detach ourselves from our past. We cannot decline our future.

This awful religion of ours still cries " On!" and

still cries "Up!" Duty, obligation, work, endurance! "No rest," you ask me? No rest, surely, in the sense we use the word here—self-indulgent laziness; certainly none for a soul not lost. Is the lost soul the soul that declines responsibility, denies obligation, refuses duty, and so has reached Nirvana?

"So many worlds! So much to do!" So far between the finite person and the infinite Person! So many princedoms to attain! So many services to do for God and the creatures of God!

Will man, the person, ever reach his highest development? "Eye hath not seen, nor ear heard," what God hath in store for His child!

Grant it is all mystery. But the mystery must contain what is good, princely, noble, manful. And what these are must be judged by the ethical judgment of the loftiest and purest and tenderest men.

Ease, reward, and the struggle ended; luxury and splendors beyond earthly dreaming; crowns, scepters, jewels, and golden houses—the noblest men care nothing for them *now*. We are Christian men. These things the barbaric kings of Ind may make *their* heaven. The Lord we serve trampled on them. We have gone so far up that our noblest trample on them too. Our reward is to *win*, to win again, and once more to *win!* Give us the victory; let who will take the triumph! The great dead singer spake the thought of men named with the conquering name of Christ:

> "Glory of virtue to fight, to struggle, to right the wrong—
> Nay, but she aimed not at glory, no lover of glory she.
> Give her the glory of going on and still to be!
> She desires no isles of the blest, no quiet seats of the just,
> To rest in a golden grove or bask in a summer sky.
> Give her the wages of going on and not to die."

Nay, the highest thing on earth conceivable to man is the human pneuma. "What know we greater than the soul?" Personality is eternal. We are ordained for our future. It demands us, and will take no refusal.

And person means obligation, duty, service. The world is a world of service. God serves and man serves. Shall not every world be a world of service?

If the "I" win on—which God wants it to do and made it to do; if it become more and more an "I," more and more a pronounced and strong "I," as it grows nearer its sole companionship, the everlasting and awful "I," shall it not find the obligations growing, the duties growing, the responsibilities growing; and shall it not find forever, as it finds now, and in all worlds, as it finds in this, that the growth comes—the development—according to the ideal pattern seen in the mount of spiritual vision, amid the thunders and lightnings of the presence of the infinite " I "—that it can only grow and only develop and only be saved from Nirvana and eternal death by facing the responsibilities, doing the duties, bending under the burdens; and with a ringing cheer of thanks for the high privilege, by accepting the everlasting law of service?

I have spoken of the doctrine of Personality—the Personality of God, the personality of man, the special, distinct peculiarity of the all-conquering religion of Jesus Christ, the Man consecrated to deliver—as an awful thing—it is; as a lonely thing—it is; as a painful, sorrowing, bitter thing—it is.

But let us not forget the end—our Lord set it before men—to become sons of God; to remain sons of God when God puts the stars out as you would snuff a candle; princes, because they have wrestled with God and men, and have won. That is the end of the law of development, according to revelation!

To become a person who is like the Personality of God—that is the end.

> "Not enjoyment and not sorrow
> Is our being's end and aim,"

but to become more and more a person who, upon the sands of the farthest shore of space, and in the midnight of wrecking worlds, can yet dare to wrestle with Almighty God, and say, "I will *not* let Thee go, except Thou bless me;" and who can, in the midst of the flaming spears of the bursting dawn, stagger on, upon the summits of the eternal hills, on flame with the eternal day, to meet the Maker, the awful "I Am that I Am," who has dwelt in the thick darkness, and so see God face to face, and *live!*

The likeness is suspicious; it has a look of forgery about it: and not unfrequently the hasty critic condemns it as such. He finds a modern air in what was really neither ancient nor modern, but a truth of every age.

The account, however, of this resemblance between distant ages and persons is not to be found in the characteristics of human nature alone. Beyond the sphere of human action and motive, in a domain which passion cannot enter, nor change of mood disturb, there is a Power by whom all the ages are controlled,—the same yesterday, to-day, and for ever. Man's folly and frailty bring him into conflict with the everlasting laws of this kingdom; and the same results of the conflict have appeared on the page of history from generation to generation since the world began. The waves of man's passionate, tumultuous life still beat against eternal barriers of right and duty: who can wonder that wreck after wreck still strews the wave-washed shore?

There are reasons, then, both in the frail nature of man, and in the unchangeable truth of the providence of God, why we should expect history to repeat itself. It must needs have its typical persons and events, its ideal characters and recurring forms of thought. You might have expected, perhaps, that knowledge of the past would save men from making old mistakes again. But it is not so: each generation, it seems, must buy its own experience by its own failures; composite characters do not throw off the elements of weakness which erewhile belonged to the same type, retaining only what is strong and pure: strength and weakness reappear together. Not in particular families only, but in nations—nay, in regions of history altogether unconnected by inherited tradition or descent—the old is still the parent of the new.

Freely admitting all this, I ask again, is there not in the saints and patriarchs, of whom your preachers are to speak, a typical character altogether their own? We Christians have our attention called to them as to no other company of men. Each name that is placed before you, has been named by our Lord or His Apostles, and enshrined for ever in the New Testament page. It is our Lord Himself who has spoken of the days of Noah, as of a familiar time,—who has recognised in Moses a Divine lawgiver—has put such honour upon Abraham, Isaac, and Jacob, as to make them a kind of hosts to welcome others into the kingdom of God. It is He who gives testimony to the righteousness of Abel, and to the faith of Abraham. If we had never heard of the Pentateuch, we should have gained the knowledge of these saints from the discourse of Christ. He does not speak of other histories, nor teach us to acquaint ourselves with the great men who have been famous in other fields of renown. Something there is in these ancients, more than in other men, which makes them fit subjects of contemplation to Jesus Christ, and therefore to the disciples of Jesus Christ in every age. For in every age they have been the honoured companions of devout Christians. They are of no school or party: no special theology dares claim them for its own. The highest art has lovingly and humbly striven to represent them: the common people use their names in familiar talk. All communions have recognised their ancient dignity: divines of all persuasions entertain their memory as the remembrance of friends. Depending on no formal act of canonization, needing no special ecclesiastical homage, they belong to the Church of all periods, and enter into the religious thought of every age. Something there must be, I say, in the great heroes of the sacred story, which makes them, in these last days, no less than in bygone centuries, fit objects for the reverent regard of the whole Christian world. In what does this fitness consist?

It is but a partial answer that we give, when we say that they won this regard from Christ by their faith. Eminent, indeed, they were by their faith: they could not else have received honour from Him at all. They had a perception of God's presence, and of His dealings both with themselves and with the world wherein they lived, to which others were strangers. Noah was building the ark while the whole race of men slumbered in careless unbelief. Abraham journeyed on towards an unknown home, while his kinsfolk stayed by their idols in the land of their birth. Moses preferred exile and affliction to a palace, although his people could scarcely be roused even to wish for escape from servitude and toil. No doubt there was a religiousness and godliness of character in them, unknown to the majority of men then, unknown to the majority of men ever since. You feel its presence even in such an one as Jacob, whose character was not without grievous stains, nor his life free from great faults. Yet he carries about with him a sense of the presence of God, refers his actions to God, dreams of Him in the hours of rest, sets up memorials of Him as he goes on his way in the world. In the less mingled character of Joseph what a marvellous reflection of Divine influences we behold! The confiding candour and loving obedience of his youth, his gentleness in suffering, his unsullied purity in time of dangerous temptation, his discretion and modesty in great office, his affectionate remembrance of father and home, his persistent charity and tenderness of heart even in old age;—look at this character, and doubt, if you can, whose image and superscription it bears. These are God's gracious gifts: they could not be possessed by one who had not a special relation to the Giver of all good. If everything prospered in Joseph's hand, it was God's blessing, be sure of it, that gave such prosperity,—God's favour that preserved, untainted, a child's purity and gentleness in the despotic ruler of a mighty land.

Yet, after all, this is (as I said) only a partial answer to the question proposed. God set His seal to these Saints, not only—or perhaps chiefly—in making them saints by His grace, but in fashioning them after a singular type, and so ordering their offices and actions as to express great truths especially connected with Himself. This is so evident in the instances of Adam, Melchisedec, and Aaron, as scarcely to need mention. But it is true also in cases less evident than these. It pleased God so to frame and fashion their lives, and to give them such opportunities,—sometimes such trials, —as to make them significant, if not to their own times, or to themselves, yet to later times and to enlightened eyes, of the principal articles of Christian doctrine. They set forth to us the acts and offices of Christ: or they explain to us God's dealings with His Church: or they illustrate the life of God in the believer's soul. They are typical, not merely as in general history events or persons foreshadow like events and persons hereafter to be reproduced, but by Divine ordinance and peculiar adaptation to an appointed end. Men call us fanciful, when we thus speak; but why should it be thought incredible that God should deal providentially with the work of His own hands? It is admitted that virtue and holiness are endowments from Him: these saints could not have lived and died as they did, but by His informing and overruling grace. If He gave them this primary and essential characteristic, why should He not also order their lives so as to express other features of His great design for man? His divine power conformed them to Himself in righteousness; did it need power more than divine to make their doings types and patterns in other respects of His own fore-ordained acts? This probability needs no postulate, but the postulate that God is the providential governor of the world. It will follow that He might have been expected to signalize the most solemn and important acts of His administration beforehand. Especially if His only-begotten Son was pleased to visit His lost world, —surely the one incomparably greatest event that could possibly come to pass in it,—He would prepare men in a thousand ways for the day of His coming. Heralds would go before the Almighty King. Type and prophecy, vision and dream, would multiply on His path: the hearts of the faithful would be stirred: a favourable opinion (as we say) would be created: men would be familiarized with words and deeds akin to those of the coming Prince: history would have its pregnant analogies, human life its intimations and foreshadowings of its Author's great design. The family, of which He was to be born, would be the guardian of these oracles, the chosen depository of these hints. Looking back along the line of its ancestry, we should expect to meet with tokens of His relation to it: the portraits of its worthies would, sometimes at least, bring His countenance before our eyes. If I do not speak now of rites and ceremonies expressly instituted by God, and directly—I had almost said, professedly—illustrating the future Gospel, it is because these form a branch of the great subject before us, which it is not our purpose to submit to you now. It is of typical *persons* that you are to hear this Lent: our preachers will bring before you in detail what I have suggested as belonging to the general view. The conviction will grow upon you, that these are not names picked out at random from the annals of the elder world, but a series of men with whom God was marvellously dealing for our sakes. You will recognise a divine idea in the whole story of their race. Perhaps you may even come to perceive that you owe portions of your own Christian knowledge to the teaching they have given you. Your idea of Christ would be less complete—to say no more—if you had not these typical antecedents of Him, and you may enjoy the hope, as you still proceed in this study, that you may gain new fruits of sacred learning: that, while you contemplate the lives of the servants, you may know more and more of the life and character of their Lord.

This, indeed, is the reason why we commend this subject to you in the season of Lent. I will not weary you with arguments to prove that *some* enlargement of your ordinary study of sacred things is proper to this consecrated time. You feel, I am sure, if you have any desire to win a blessing from its due observance, that its call to you includes this duty,—the duty of reading more, or thinking more, about Him whom you seek. Some additional meditation, or reading, or hearing of sermons, has formed part of every scheme of religious exercises in Lent. With you, my brethren in Christ, it will not, I trust, be only part of a scheme of exercises, but a real help to that growth in grace, to which you desire and pray to attain. The very discipline of rigorously claiming an additional portion of each day, however small, for the thought of God, will be of effectual service to you. You want deliverance from the world in which you live. You feel that it has more power over you than it ought to have: it is not merely a world around you—that must be so—but within you. You are too apt to think its thoughts, and adopt its principles, without so much as considering whether they are good and true. With some of you, perhaps, there is an overwhelming influence of this kind : the duties, or the pleasures of life, are so many and so incessant, that you have, or seem to have, no time ever to question yourselves on the grounds of your opinions or the motives of your conduct,—no space for retirement, or any place in which you can commune with your God. Lent gives you such a time,—bids you find such a place.

The outline of these Sermons may suggest to you one profitable subject, at least, on which to exercise your thoughts. Considered as mere history, it might transport you far from present excitements and every-day thoughts. The contemplation of that far-off Eastern world, with its grave fathers spending long generations in the seriousness of the old patriarchal life, might of itself lessen your absorbing admiration for the busy, restless Western society of modern days. The thought of the greatest of them all, " a mighty prince," as the children of Heth called him, yet " a stranger and sojourner," living simply in his tent a quiet pastoral life, rebukes our self-indulgent, luxurious existence, with its complicated engagements, and its thousand needless cares. But all this is the least part of the great subject before you. Abraham rejoiced to see the day of Christ. His thoughts and hopes were fixed on a power and a glory yet to come. You are privileged to enter into those thoughts, but with a clearer knowledge, and with an abounding thankfulness, of which he had only the elements and anticipations within his reach. Communing in spirit with Abraham, Isaac, and Jacob, you are communing with those who longed for Christ, who are with Christ in glory now. You come back from their society as the disciples came down from the Mount, when they had heard Moses and Elias talking with their Lord. You have a glory shining above you, a reflection of heavenly society, a fragrance of Paradise. You have been with the Saints : you have drawn, through their converse, nearer to Christ. Let this be the aim of all your contemplation —to approach more closely to Him. Brethren, this is the great purpose of Lent ; the great purpose of every season, of every devotional exercise, every holy meditation, to make you know and love your Divine Master more. What reason you will have to thank God when the bright Easter morning dawns upon you, if by these, or any other, meditations, humbly entertained, faithfully pursued, you have been led to gain a clearer insight into the perfection of His holiness, the depth of His redeeming love. Life, when we come to the end of it, will be reckoned by these recurring years, and seasons, and times of grace. Let not one of these pass—oh, let not this one pass,—without its own fresh gain of heavenly thoughts received and cherished, its own fresh earnest of the hope to be with Abraham, Isaac, and Jacob, in the kingdom of God.

SERMON II.

Adam.

ROMANS v. 14.

"Who is the figure of Him that was to come."

ὅς ἐστι τύπος τοῦ μέλλοντος.

"Qui est forma futuri."

I ASSUME that there can be no doubt as to the meaning of the words which we render, "Him that was to come;" and that the ambiguity to which the Latin version, *Qui est forma futuri**, might have possibly lent itself, can have no place in the original. In Adam, the Apostle's phrase leads us to see, not the likeness of *what was to be*, but the Figure of *Him that was to come*. Doubtless, we may read in Adam the foreshadowing of what was to happen in the world, of the future of his race; but here, the Apostle speaks of the First Man as the Type of a Person, the First Type of Jesus Christ the Lord.

We are accustomed to this way of speaking, and often it hardly arrests our thought. And yet it might; for between Type and Antitype, in this case, the relation appears at first sight that of the extremest opposition of condition and character, and resulting work and consequences. "As in Adam all die, so in Christ shall all be made alive." "The first man is of the earth, earthy; the second, is the Lord from Heaven." What oppo-

* Vid. Aug. Epist. clvii. 20; De Pecc. Mer., i. 13, iii. 9.

sition can be greater? Yet Adam is the Type of Christ. He, in whom we see the whole history of our sin and the true image of our falling short, is the figure of Him in whom is summed up all our hope of righteousness and the whole promise of our completeness. He who stands at the head of the history of this world, —so strange, so dark, so short,—is the figure of the "Father of the everlasting Age to come." He of whom, in the utter dimness of the beginning of time, we in vain attempt to form a conception, stands as the type of that Brother and Friend whose words and ways and mind are ever open to us, and whom we can know and love as we can none other, who has been among us and has gone from us. He who had a great trust and betrayed it so lightly is the type of Him who came to do His Father's will, and was obedient, even unto death. By what common likeness can we join together him in whom we behold the Fall, with Him in whom we receive the great and eternal Restoration? How can the great failure be the type of the great victory? the great transgression, of the great forgiveness; the great disaster, of the great recovery; fatal defeat and fault, of fulfilment and perfection? Every figure must in some respects be a contrast; and conversely, every contrast implies a parallel and correspondence; but here, the contrast seems to extinguish the likeness. How is darkness to be the figure of light? sin, of righteousness? death, of life? How should the beginning of the downward road of evil reflect the beginning of the new creation of righteousness? how should the Creature, in his first misery and weakness, suggest and represent the Creator, Holy and Strong—"the Lord from Heaven," dwelling among us in His awful Power and Love, to reverse our doom?

But high and low lie very near to one another, in that order in which the First Man and the Second are made by St. Paul to be answering counterparts. It is in a world where things are less real, where our thoughts are swayed by opinion and half knowledge and custom, that we shrink from putting them together, except as opposites. But the wisdom of God, which sees all things from end to end in the infinite vastness of the dispensation of grace, has no such restraint. In the first man, in the depth of his fall, it traces the lineaments of that Holy One who was in the fulness of time to bear his flesh and blood. He who made man was not ashamed of him. He who made man did not disdain to share the necessities of his humiliation, accepted the community of his loss and shame. He bore man's likeness; He grudged not that man should bear His own; that man, in the very moment of his overthrow, should be the prophecy of his Deliverer. He was not ashamed that we should see, in him in whom the world was lost, reflections of His own peculiar glory, the image and the promise of what He was Himself to make perfect. In the very beginning of human history and destiny, we find the figure of its fulfilment, which yet was to be so different.

We see in the great type of the Apostle two things. He to whom, step by step, our blood goes back, he in whom were the germs of all that we are, is set before us as the eternal memorial, at once of what man was meant for, and of what man has become. In him are seen together, the intention and the swerving, the purpose and the disappointment. He stands not alone in this melancholy significance. The Bible has many such types of good made frustrate, and the actual world is full of them. But in Adam it is the fortunes of mankind that we see summed up. He stands for us all; for all living souls, who from generation to generation receive and hand on the breath of human life. In him is the image of all his seed. His is no mere personal calling, no mere personal fall, like those of Saul and Judas. Meant for what he was, even man's perfection, yet in his mortality and pain, though brought upon him by himself, he makes his mute but undoubting appeal for restoration; he witnesses that all has not been in vain, that he was not made for nought. Where the glimpse that is given us is of the destinies of mankind, there, where the purpose and the failure come together, they seem to demand the remedy, and to announce it. So those, whose thoughts are moulded by the Spirit of the God of Hope, instinctively gather: so, the Bible, from first to last the comforter and upholder of human hope, bids them believe that their thoughts are true. He in whom we fell is the Figure of Him that was to come, because he faintly shadows forth the unimaginable perfection reserved for human nature in its true Head; and because, in the depths of his own ruin and failure, he cries out and stretches forth his hands for the fulfilment of what he has missed; and by those cries and yearnings to the Father who made him, is the warrant and promise of it. The type of our lost estate, to all experience irrecoverable, the type of our common disaster which once seemed as if it might have alleviations, but no reversal, is transfigured, while we gaze, into an image, faint yet surrounded with titles of awful honour, of One in whom the obstinate longings of man were to be more than made good; one by whom the "creature," long "subject to vanity, should be delivered from the bondage of corruption into the glorious liberty of the children of God." For the First man stands at the head of the genealogy of the Second, as "Adam, which was the Son of God." The First man has that awful thing said of him which is said of the Second, in however more ineffable a meaning,—"In the image of God, made He man;"—the Son, "Who is the Image of the invisible God," "the express image of His person."

In Adam we have announced to us the archetype of man; what was the design of his being, what was the end and original law of his nature:—"Let us make man in our image, after our likeness;" "So God created man in His own image: in the image of God created He him." In Adam, we are told at the very opening of the Bible of the unity and brotherhood of mankind, that last discovery, long fought against and hardly recognised, of the widening thought of ages, of the conspiring feelings and reason of civilized man. In Adam, we have that position of man as the crown of all that we know, which is so absolutely unique and overwhelmingly mysterious—as the bondsman and victim of nature, yet its lord; in all its infinite spaces, the one thing free[b]; free to choose, free to obey, free to

---

[b] "The first appearance of man in nature was the appearance of a new being in nature. ... The sun had risen, and the sun descended, the stars looked down upon the earth, the mountains climbed to heaven, the cliffs stood upon the shore, the same as now, countless ages before a single being existed who saw it. The counterpart of this whole scene was wanting,—the understanding mind: that mirror in which the whole was to be reflected; and when this arose, it was a new birth for creation itself, that it became *known*—an image in the mind of a conscious being. But even consciousness and knowledge were a less strange and miraculous introduction into the world than *conscience*. ... Mysterious in his entrance into this scene, man is *now* an insulation in it. ... What can be more incomprehensible, more heterogeneous, a more ghostly resident in nature, than the sense of right and wrong? What is it? whence is it? The obligation of man to sacrifice himself for right is a truth which springs out of an abyss, the mere attempt to look down into which confuses the reason. Man is alone, then, in nature; he alone of all the creatures communes with

rise; endowed, he alone of things here, with the wonderful power of self-conquest, self-correction, self-improvement; with capacities infinite of drawing nearer and nearer for ever to the Father, in whose Image he was made; the one thing able to know God, and to know what to God is good,—the one among creatures here whose perfection lay in the perfection of his *will*, in owning the sway of those strange, awful words, *ought*, and *ought not*.

And that was the prerogative and calling which was cast away. That was the purpose which was made void. That was the place in the order of God's creation, which from that time to this the race has not fulfilled. In this image of what man was made for begins the terrible record of what man has been; the unfolding of that terrible and almost infinite variety of failure and sin which crowds the pages of human history, and is its first and deepest impression. "In Adam all die:" nothing remains unspoilt; no promise reaches its true fulfilment, no good abides without decay and degeneracy: all wears out,—evil, happily, too, or the world would perish,—but also good. "In Adam all die:" we see it in man's greatest types as in his lowest; we see it in his refinement and in his degradation; we see it in his politics and in his Churches, as well as in those monstrous aggregations of unorganized men, without law, without country, without home, which crowd the outskirts of our great cities. Even in all those great doings of his, so elevating, so hopeful, of which the world is full, yet there lurks the taint of the heart not whole and the will infirm: and on them all

---

a Being out of nature; and he divides himself from all other physical life by prophesying, in the face of universal visible decay, his own immortality."—*Mozley, Bampton Lectures*, iii. pp. 88, 89.

waits death, breaking off the great labour of good, beating down the great triumphs over evil and folly. And what are these great labourers, great conquerors, whose work, too, has to begin afresh when they go,— what are these few among the so many, who "as soon as they are born, begin to draw to their end, and have no sign of virtue to shew?" Take the men and women, as we meet them in the streets; take the huge multitudes of the average; leave out the extremes on both sides,—extremes are rare in all orders of things, though they are less rare on the low side than on the high;— and what a spectacle rises before our mind, of falling short of standards, of things marred, of misuse, of emptiness, of decay. Think only, in all generations of time, in all countries of mankind, of the *waste of life;* of what to us, at least, can only seem the waste of life; the waste of life wantonly cut short, the waste of life, *itself wasted* in the having; the wastes of savage idleness; the wastes of barbarian wars and destructions:—life wasted in the artificial vices and wants of the highest social state; the waste of life, in *men*, for war, and, it must be said, for much that we call industry; the waste of life, in *women*, who live for man's sin, and by it. These, we know, are things on a great scale; they are things accepted, as what cannot be helped, as what in the nature of things must be. Do they not reveal to us a world in which, *who can tell how much*, life is wasted; wasted by men for themselves, wasted by what others do with them. "One day telleth another, and one night certifieth another;" and the tale they repeat is the same dreary story, of to-day fruitless as yesterday, of to-morrow sure to be thrown away as to-day; of irremediable, continuing *waste*. In such things as these we see, in its true measure, what is meant by the Fall.

Is not so manifest a purpose, and so manifest a falling short, the very ground and prophecy of hope? I do not suppose that we can always argue from tendency to effect; that every unfulfilled promise, and capacity, and aspiration, implies at last its fulfilment. But there are failures which are final, and there are failures which, in the very moment of their ill-success,—by what they *might* do, by what they *do*,—carry with them the promise of being at last repaired. The fall of Sodom was not like the fall of Israel, or the going astray of Greece and Rome. And here, in Adam and the race he stands for,—amid ruin, amid incredible debasement, amid the very mysteries of iniquity and apostasy around him, amid horrors not to be exaggerated, not to be told, of his history,—still are to be discerned the outlines of the image of God. Can that image stay with men, and not be to them the pledge of remedy? Can that image strike its print so deep,—can the dream of nature, contradicted everywhere, yet be always and obstinately of goodness, of what is noblest, and purest, and most divine,—and not lift mankind to the looking-for of deliverance, of that day when the old shall pass, and all things be made new? Can man feel, as he must feel, that sin is not his fate, that evil is not his natural law,— and not find in the power within him, of correcting what is amiss, of repentance, of improvement, the irresistible argument of hope? Surely, from Adam's Creation and Adam's Fall, from such a purpose and such an overthrow, did not the cry go up, prophetic of the grace that listened to it, for retrieval, for a new beginning? "In Adam all die,"—Adam, who was "made in the image and likeness of God." Is it not reason, indeed, that from that time till now, " the whole creation," in him made subject to vanity, "groaneth and travaileth in pain together," crying out to be redeemed; not accepting as its fate "the bondage of corruption;" earnestly expecting the accomplishment of a destiny too great to fail at last? Is not this the expostulation and plea of our nature,—in its deep humiliation, in its unconquerable consciousness of what it was meant for and in *whose* hand it lives,—

> " O remember what my substance is;
> The work of Thy hands;
> The likeness of thy countenance.
> Despise not Thou the work of Thine own hands:
> Hast Thou made for nought Thine own image and likeness?
> For nought, if Thou destroy it [c]."

Human nature,—in what it is, and in what it is not; in what it would be and cannot be; in its aims and its incompleteness; in its stateliness and its deformity; in its charm and its repulsiveness; in its power and its failure,—sends up the cry for restoration. Man, but a link in the chain of nature, may stretch forth hands in vain to laws which cannot hear and cannot change. But can man, *the Spirit*, cry to the God who made him, the Father of Spirits, the Living, the All-compassionate, the True, without the prayer for help and redemption being itself the pledge of its fulfilment?

And thus, in his double character, of greatness and of misery; of the greatness of his end and the misery of his state; in his longings and their disappointment, in his wish for good and inability to resist the present, in the eternal conflict of conscience and passion, in the strange humiliation of a real *will*, ever defeated and defeating itself; in all the astonishing and deep contradictions of his condition, his desires, his history, he

[c] Bishop Andrewes.

foreshadows and foretells the deliverance which corresponds at once to the awful height of what he was meant for, and the depth, beyond our measuring, to which he had sunk. For his Deliverer was one like himself; yet with all the difference that there is between the Creature and the Creator. He who "took hold" of him was He who made him,—after whose Image he was made, whose Likeness he was meant to attain to: greater none could be, to stamp and make certain the greatness of his nature. But who can tell the depth of the humiliation of the Second Adam? "The Lord from heaven," the "quickening Spirit" by whom the dead are made alive, the "Word made flesh;" what was He but the likeness of His creature, in the wretchedness in which he had gone forth from Paradise; in the "form of a servant," in "the likeness of sinful flesh;" seeking the lost in the company of the lowest of the lost; the friend of "publicans and sinners," accepting the reproach of their companionship; tempted and scorned, a man of sorrows and acquainted with grief; bearing in the eyes of the world all the marks of ignominious and unsuccessful sin; judged, in the name of the Highest, as a deceiver and a blasphemer; made sin for us, made a curse for us; forsaken of God, a worm and no man, the very scorn of men, and outcast of the people. What has man done of worst evil, of which the apparent shadow did not rest on his Deliverer? What unrest, what pain, what privation, troubles his lot, which his Deliverer did not share? what is there in the sinner's doom at the Fall —shame, sorrow, death—which the Sinless does not accept, in order, in accepting it, to reverse it? Face to face with the amazing contrarieties of the Fall are the amazing contrarieties of the Incarnation. Face to face with the greatness and the misery of the First man, are the greatness and the misery of the Second.

And so, at the point where the Fall leaves man, Redemption meets him: and the meeting-point is at the lowest depths. The Fall left him a being of mysterious and surmised greatness, but of most real and visible distance from all that he seemed made for; struggling with corruption and sin, or sinking under them; struggling with disaster, struggling with pain, struggling vainly with death; ever haunted by dreams of perfection, by dreams of bliss, and by the waking certainty of wretchedness and vanity. Whatever else may be true about him, what is palpable is, *his humiliation*. And then, in the very point of deepest ignominy and disorder, starting from all its disadvantages, traversing its paths, surrounded by all its badges, reflecting its dreary colours, not refusing the semblances of its more real evil; amid that mortal confusion and degradation of conscience, in which good is taken for evil, and evil for good, and in which the Holiest was thought the vilest of sinners,—the Restorer of man begins His new and strange work, His new creation. In Adam we see what Christ was to meet with, and to begin with; where Adam had descended to, Christ descended to meet him: in sorrow, in infirmity, in defeat, in the humiliations of mortality, in all but the evil of our treacherous *will*, man's partner: his partner in such anguish as is described in the Psalms; in daily company with his distresses and all that train of unknown and nameless suffering which surrounds the Son of Man in the Gospels. The work of heaven, it begins on earth, amid the too well known conditions of our state, the too well known and familiar realities of what we are and what we have to go through. From that which seems to be but the continuation of the doom of the Fall, from that which seems to be its aggravation in the person of the Innocent, from the darkness and dreary gloom with which Adam's history closes, issues forth the power which is to repair the wreck, the light which is to make it no longer hopeless, the Life which is to quicken the dead. The figure is fulfilled; its conflicting aspects are reconciled in the transcendent Antitype. "In Adam all die: in Christ shall all be made alive;" but not before the death of the First man is repeated in the Second; not before "God had made Him to be sin for us who knew no sin, that we might be made the righteousness of God in Him;" not before the "Captain of man's salvation should by the grace of God taste death for every man;" "should be made perfect through sufferings."

Adam is "the Figure of Him that was to come," the figure of our perfection, and of our ruin and mortality; the figure of God's intention, of what man has spoiled and God repaired. We may measure the reality of the deliverance by the reality, which we know, of the wreck; we may measure the vastness of what was wrecked by the greatness of the remedy[d]. And so the world is changed, and what might but be guessed at before is made certain now. We are of a race that had lost its way; and now we know it. We are of a race whose prospects and destiny it is vain to circumscribe by what we see; it belongs to a world to which this world cannot reach, and where we are linked with God. So even the First man dared to imagine before the Second came; but he knew not, and all the practical energy of his nature was directed _here_. He went forth and did great things. As it is said in those

[d] Pascal, Pensées, ii. 85, 145 (ed. Faugère).

great Choruses which are the Psalms of Heathenism,—
he subdued the earth, he founded states, he sought
out arts, he mastered powers living and powers elemental, he found the secret of beauty, and the spell
of words, and the power of numbers, and the fine threads
that waken and order thought ; he made the world his
workshop, his arsenal, his palace ; generation after generation he learned to know more of its inexhaustible
magnificence, to use more of its inexhaustible gifts ;
his eye was more opened, his sense more delicate, his
hand more crafty ; he created, he measured, he gathered together, he enjoyed. He is before us now, in
his greatness, his hopes, his pride, with even nobler
aims and vaster tasks, alleviating misery, curing injustice, bridling or extinguishing disease. But still he
is the First Man : of the riddle of his nature he has not
the key, and despairs of reaching it : he passes in his
greatness, and never continueth in one stay : sorrow and
decay baffle him, sin entangles him, and at the end is
death. "Of the earth, earthy ;" of the earth, bounded
by its barriers, invisible, impassable. And now, side by
side with him, is the Second Man, from the Manger, the
Cross, the Grave,—dead, yet alive, and alive for ever :
attended by His train of sanctities, by unthought-of
revelations of heart, by the "things of the Spirit," by
hopes and peace which for this world were an idle
dream, by the new Beatitudes. He comes in the greatness of his strength, he comes in weakness : but strength
and weakness to Him are both alike ; for love, which is
of God, in strong and weak, is the life of the new creation, its "one thing needful," the essential mark of its
presence. So He comes, on the bed of sickness, in the
lifelong burden, in the broken heart ; with the children
in spirit, the poor, the feeble, the helpless, the unknown ;

with the sorrows of penitence, the hunger after righteousness, the longings to be true, the longings to be pure, the joy of forgiveness, the hope that is for the other side of the grave. Strange attendants for the company of the Deliverer; but they bring with them the victory which nothing else has gained. "The First Man is of the earth, earthy; the Second Man is the Lord from heaven." O Soul of man,—called to this wonderful existence, so gifted, yet so rigidly bounded: made for such great things, yet turned aside by such poor ones: so promising, yet so transient: the breath of a day between the two eternities, yet rich with power, and thought, and beauty, rich in capacities of grace and goodness, ever unfolding, ever growing; conscious of such needs and such evils, longing for such firm reality and truth, responding to such calls, and then going hence, as if never having been:—where is to be thy part? what wilt thou do with what is given thee, with that great and fearful thing which we call life? Wilt thou rest in the portion of the First Adam:—great, lovely, as it often is, merely to live, to see, to be glad in the sky above and God's blessing on the earth, in our home, in our work? It is enough, if we had no more; it is enough to be thankful for, if our view closed here. "But the First Man is of the earth, earthy: and there is the Second Man, the Lord from heaven." And none but He dares claim the two great victories: the victory over sin, the victory over death. With Him only is it said, "O wretched man that I am, who shall deliver me from the body of this death? I thank God, through Jesus Christ our Lord." With Him only it is said, "that this corruptible must put on incorruption, and this mortal must put on immortality." Only He speaks to us here, of "mortality swallowed up of life."

With Him only it is said, "The sting of death is sin, and the strength of sin is the law: but thanks be to God, who giveth us the victory through our Lord Jesus Christ." He only

> "Holds for us the keys of either home,
> Earth and the world to come [e]."

O Soul of man, inheritor of the First Adam, new-born to the Second, which wilt thou choose?

[e] Lyra Apostolica, No. 71.

SERMON III.
Abel.

HEBREWS xi. 4.

"By faith Abel offered unto God a more excellent sacrifice than Cain, by which he obtained witness that he was righteous, God testifying of his gifts: and by it he, being dead, yet speaketh."

ACCORDING to the appointed course of these Lenten Sermons, it falls to my lot this evening to speak to you of the first martyr recorded in the world's history, of him to whom Divine wisdom has applied the noble epithet of "RIGHTEOUS ABEL[a]." I have to dwell upon his history both in its general aspect and in its typical relation to the Gospel, and to shew you how the message which he thus delivered is an abiding message of comfort and instruction to the Church of God, even to the end of the world.

We find the circumstances of Abel's history, so far as they are handed down to us, in the fourth chapter of the Book of Genesis. We there read that after the expulsion from Paradise, Eve bare to Adam a son, whom she at once named Cain, or "acquisition," saying, perhaps with a reference to the first promise, "I have gotten," or acquired, "a man from the Lord." We are then told that "she again bare his brother, Abel." The names of remarkable persons in Holy

---

[a] St. Matt. xxiii. 35.

Scripture are frequently given to them, as by a Divine instinct, at the time of their coming into the world, to mark something peculiar, either in the circumstances of their birth, or in their future destinies. But whether or not Abel received this appellation at his birth, his name, which signifies "vanity," or "nothingness," is strikingly indicative of the frailty and shortness of his life, and of his sudden and violent end.

Well; the two brothers grew up, and in due time entered, each of them, upon their allotted callings in life. Of Cain we read that he "tilled the ground." It was a part of the Divine sentence inflicted upon Adam that the ground was cursed for his sake, and that thenceforth it would yield nothing of what was precious and useful, but in return for hard and toilsome labour. It was not, indeed, that there was no labour in Paradise, for we are told that the Lord God put Adam into the garden of Eden "to dress it and to keep it." A Divine hand first planted and adorned the garden, and thenceforth it was Adam's business, by his own industry, to maintain its primitive beauty. Thus industry was demanded of man, as of all God's creatures, even in his state of innocency. And hence the curse inflicted upon man was the curse, not of labour, but of painful and oppressive labour. "In the sweat of his face he was to eat bread;" and so, as has been well observed, "we were designed for labour in our first happy state; and upon our lapse thence were further doomed to it, as the sole remedy of our needs, and of the inconveniences to which we became exposed [b]."

Thus Cain became a husbandman. But Abel followed another pursuit, which, though not exempting from activity and vigilance, afforded more opportunity

[b] Barrow, vol. iii. p. 206.

for thought and contemplation ^c. While Cain was "subduing the earth," Abel was asserting the dominion which God had given to man over the beasts of the field, and he became a "keeper of sheep." We need not enter into the question whether the flesh of animals was ever used for food before the Flood. It is sufficient for our purpose to remember that the wool and the milk of the flock would be required for purposes of clothing and of food, to say nothing of those higher typical uses to which I shall have presently to call your attention.

We next read that "in process of time," or rather "at the end or fulfilment of days," as the words might be rendered, "Cain brought of the fruit of the ground an offering to the Lord; and Abel, he also brought of the firstlings of his flock, and of the fat thereof." It is possible that this religious service may have taken place upon the occasion of some appointed festival or solemn anniversary^d, and that thus the time as well as the place of offering may have been of Divine appointment. But, however this may be, the two brothers bring, each of them, their offerings, the gifts in either case being characteristic of their different employments. The husbandman, Cain, brings of "the fruit of the ground;" the shepherd, Abel, brings of the "firstlings of his flock." Perhaps the words of the narrative may imply that Abel took more pains than Cain in the selection of

---

^c "In the first event or occurrence after the fall of man, we see, as the Scriptures have infinite mysteries, not violating at all the truth of the story or letter, an image of the two estates, the contemplative state and the active state, figured in the two persons of Abel and Cain, and in the two simplest and most primitive trades of life, that of the shepherd, who, by reason of his leisure, rest in a place, and living in view of heaven, is a lively image of a contemplative life; and that of the husbandman; where we see again the favour and election of God went to the shepherd, and not to the tiller of the ground."—*Bacon, Advancement of Learning*, bk. i.

^d Perhaps on the seventh day, or Sabbath.

his gifts. But even if the words convey this meaning, we can hardly find here a sufficient reason why the oblation of one brother should have found favour rather than that of the other[e]. Nevertheless, we are told immediately that "the Lord had respect unto Abel and to his offering; but unto Cain and to his offering He had not respect." In the one case, both the person and his offering were acceptable to Jehovah; in the other case, both were alike distasteful to Him. And then we read that "Cain was very wroth, and his countenance fell." Whatever defects there may have been, whether in his disposition or in the nature of his offering, (and it would seem from the narrative that there was something faulty in both,) it is at least plain that he valued the favour of God; for as soon as he perceived that his offering was rejected, he was overcome with anger and vexation. But notwithstanding his exhibition of sullen displeasure, his Maker condescended to reason with him: "Why art thou wroth? and why is thy countenance fallen? If thou doest well, shalt thou not be accepted? and if thou doest not well, sin lieth at the door. And unto thee shall be his desire, and thou shalt rule over him." If I may venture to paraphrase this

---

[e] The Talmud supposes that Cain offered not his *best* produce. This view is held by several of the Fathers, as St. Ambrose and St. Chrysostom. Cornelius à Lapide says, "Obtulit Cain de fructibus terræ, secundos scilicet et viliores fructus. Primos igitur et meliores fructus sibi reservabat Cain; opponitur enim Abelo, qui obtulit Deo primogenita, et de adipibus, id est optima et pinguissima gregis sui."
To the same purpose, Milton:—
"thither anon
A sweaty reaper from his tillage brought
Firstfruits, the green ear, and the yellow sheaf
Unculled, as came to hand; a shepherd next
More meek, came with the firstlings of his flock
Choicest and best."
Paradise Lost, bk. xi. l. 433.

remonstrance, it may probably be thus understood :—
" Thou hast displeased Me, both by thy offering and by the spirit with which thou hast made it. But if thou wilt henceforth do good, and follow My revealed will, thou mayest even yet find acceptance, like Abel; but if not, remember that sin lieth at the door; it is close at hand, lying in wait for thee, crouching like a wild beast of prey, ready to spring upon thee. Nevertheless, if thou wilt even now follow My commands, though sin is desirous to have thee, thou mayest even yet rule over it[f]." Thus this remonstrance was an admonition to Cain to submit himself to God's will, and to banish from his mind those turbulent passions of envy and discontent which were then agitating him. He was in great danger, but he might yet escape. It was not too late. It was still in his power to obtain a triumph. If he could not altogether destroy the enemy sin, he might at least hold it in check, and arrest its progress.

Perhaps for a time this merciful expostulation had its effect. The narrative, here as elsewhere, is somewhat obscure, though it seems to imply that there may have been a temporary reconciliation[g]. But within a while sin revived; the old feeling of envy and hatred

---

[f] This interpretation is favoured by St. Ambrose, St. Jerome, St. Augustine, and others of the Fathers; also by Cornelius à Lapide, Kalisch, Wordsworth, &c. Lightfoot and others consider "sin" in this passage to mean "a sin-offering," but it is difficult to reconcile this meaning with the context.

[g] Kalisch, following Gesenius, says that verse 8 might be rendered "And Cain said *it* to Abel his brother," that is, he communicated to him the words of God, which confidence might be regarded as shewing a disposition towards reconciliation. There is, however, some good authority for the Septuagint addition, "And Cain said unto Abel his brother, 'Let us go into the field.'" See Canon Selwyn's article on the Septuagint in Smith's "Bible Dictionary."

gained ascendancy, and in a moment of overpowering passion, perhaps when Abel was reasoning with him of the promises of redemption and of judgment to come, "Cain rose up against him and slew him."

Such is the narrative as we read it in Genesis. There is no lack of testimony in the New Testament to its actual historical reality; while for its typical meaning we can hardly find a more helpful passage than that which I have chosen for my text, it being carefully remembered that one great design of this Epistle to the Hebrews is to shew the relation of the ancient sacrifices to Christ[h].

Now in this text the Apostle tells us that "by faith Abel offered unto God a more excellent sacrifice than Cain." The expression, "a more excellent sacrifice," is very remarkable. An early translation quaintly but accurately renders it, "a much more sacrifice[i]." And the meaning is clearly this, that by faith Abel was enabled to present that which was much more of the nature of a sacrifice than that offered by Cain, and that by this he obtained witness that he was righteous; righteous, that is, in the sense of being justified by his faith, God manifesting by some visible sensible token, probably that of fire consuming the sacrifice, that He accepted the offering[k]. It is difficult to see

---

[h] "The doctrine of this Epistle plainly is, that the legal sacrifices were allusions to the great and final Atonement to be made by the Blood of Christ, and not that this was an allusion to those."—*Butler's Analogy*, part ii. c. v.

[i] That of Wycliffe.

[k] "Quæres, pro signo declaravit Deus sibi placere oblationes Abelis, non autem Cain? Respondeo; communiter tradunt Patres, Deum id igne de cœlo misso in sacrificium Abelis, non autem Cain, declarasse; ignem enim hunc combussisse et consumpsisse sacrificium Abelis, Caini vero sacrificium intactum reliquisse." "Id ipsum asserunt et tradunt S. Hier., Procopius, Cyrillus hîc, Chrysost., &c., unde et Theodotion vertit"—καὶ ἐνεπύρισεν

in what the faith of Abel could have consisted, if not in the nature of his oblation. The question, therefore, that I have to ask myself is this, What grounds had Abel for believing that this would be "a more excellent sacrifice?"

Now we know that expiatory sacrifices have been prevalent throughout the world from very early times. How, then, do we account for this? Did the institution of sacrifice take its origin from the natural reason of man, or can it be traced to some distinct primæval revelation? It may safely be assumed that a common custom, diffused amongst races of the greatest diversity, must have sprung either from human reason or from some special and definite command of the Creator. Now we can hardly conceive that reason could have originated the idea of animal sacrifices. It might, indeed, conceive the propriety of presentations to God as thank-offerings, of the fruits and flowers of earth; but it could hardly suggest, without Divine guidance, that God would be pleased with the blood of animals and the fat of slain beasts, at least for their own sake. I admit that the institution once existing, the human conscience would acquiesce in its fitness, because there is that in fallen man which tells him that he is impure. The sense of sin prompts him to hide himself from the presence of the Lord. It tells him that there is something wrong between him and his Maker, and that this wrong needs to be redressed. But the question is, whether the unassisted reason of man could have devised such a method of reconciliation as this. To this there is apparently but one answer. The conclusion seems forced upon us, that a custom so universal, and

αὐτὰ ὁ Θεός—"inflammavit Dominus super Abel et sacrificium ejus, super Cain non."—*Cornelius à Lapide, in loc.*

yet at the same time so opposed to the primary conceptions or instincts of men, must have been derived from some supernatural revelation. And it is nothing to the point to contend that these sacrifices soon degenerated to corrupt and superstitious uses. All superstition is built up upon what is true. Superstition is something excessive, which the ill-regulated or uninstructed mind adds to revealed religion. Superstition is an abuse; but every abuse pre-supposes a true and proper use.

Let us see, then, whether there are sufficient reasons for concluding that expiatory sacrifices would be ordained by God. Now we know that immediately upon the fall of man the promise was made of his recovery through Christ. In the predicted "Seed of the woman" there lay the foundation of his hopes, and in the dim twilight of that first Gospel announcement he saw the pathway of his deliverance. From that moment the coming Saviour, who in some mysterious manner was to destroy the power of sin and Satan, became the great object of his faith. But how was this faith to be kept alive in the world? how but by some outward sign, which should have a typical resemblance to the thing signified. The Being who was to bruise Satan must Himself be bruised; and thus the first promise indicated that in order to the expiation of sin there must be the shedding of blood. If, then, we believe that Christ Jesus was "fore-ordained," that He was indeed "the Lamb slain from the foundation of the world[1]," what more appropriate type of that deliverance could be appointed than that of sacrifice? Christ was to appear at the end of the world to put away sin by the one finished Sacrifice upon the Cross. But mankind

[1] Rev. xiii. 8.

must be gradually educated to receive this truth, and in this education the sacrificial system was the greatest element. These vicarious and representative sacrifices had indeed a twofold meaning. They reminded the offerer that he deserved to die on account of his sins, and at the same time they foreshadowed that death which was to be undergone by the Redeemer in the fulness of time to deliver man from the consequences of sin. Their true meaning is thus vividly expressed by Eusebius: "Whilst men had no victim that was more excellent, more precious, and more worthy of God, animals were made the price and ransom of their souls. And their substituting these animals in their own room, bore indeed some affinity to their suffering themselves, in which sense all the ancient worshippers and friends of God made use of them. The Holy Spirit had taught them that there should one day come a Victim more venerable, more holy, more worthy of God. He had likewise instructed them how to point Him out to the world by types and shadows. And thus they became prophets, and were not ignorant of their having been chosen out to represent to mankind the things which God resolved to accomplish[m]."

In real truth the great central point of Divine revelation is the Sacrifice of Jesus Christ upon the Cross. Around this, the whole of Revelation revolves. It is to this that all former sacrifices are to be referred, and in the light of this alone that they can be understood. There probably was, in those early ages, but a vague and imperfect knowledge of their typical mean-

---

[m] Eusebius, Demonst. Evang., lib. i. c. 10. "Sacrifices of expiation were commanded the Jews, and obtained amongst most other nations from tradition, whose original probably was Revelation."—*Butler's Analogy*, part ii. c. 5.

ing; but at any rate there was room for the exercise of faith, through such sacrifices, in the promise of salvation. And thus Abel's sacrifice was his parable of redemption, and in offering it he was justified sacramentally, and by faith. He had grasped the great truth of man's sinfulness and man's need of an atonement; and as he presented his lamb upon the altar he delivered a witness, the power of which no lapse of ages can weaken,—a witness to the efficacy of "that Blood which cleanseth from all sin." We thus see why Abel's offering was accepted, and why Cain's was rejected. Abel by his sacrifice proved his faith in the Divinely appointed method of salvation; whereas Cain, disdaining the Divine command, and perhaps considering the means unworthy of the end, deemed it sufficient to render his homage to God as the God of Providence. Cain sought to be accepted for his own righteousness; Abel sought acceptance through the righteousness and death of another. The question to be solved in that early period, the question which all along the ages demands an answer, was this, whether "Revelation ought to control Reason, or Reason to prescribe to Revelation[n]." Cain would accept no guide but Reason; Abel added Faith to Reason; and as the fire from heaven fell and consumed his sacrifice, there was a sensible evidence that he had found justification; and so from that primæval altar there went forth the undying message, even to the remotest depths of time, that "without shedding of blood is no remission," and that the Atoning Sacrifice upon the Cross is the only appointed means by which Death can be abolished and Sin done away.

Thus, also, this first martyr teaches us something of

[n] South.

the nature of that faith which justifies. It is not the mere assent of the understanding; it is not merely an act of the mind which follows necessarily wherever there is sufficient testimony. The faith which Abel had is not a natural gift; it is the gift of God. The great and principal object which is presented to the faith that justifies is Jesus Christ dying upon the Cross for the sins of the world. Faith contemplates this object; it accepts the truth that there is none other Name whereby we can be saved; and it inspires each faithful man with the desire of being found in Christ, not having his own righteousness, but "the righteousness which is of God by faith." Here was just the difference between these two brothers. Cain rejected the primæval revelation, but Abel accepted it. Cain was self-confident, too philosophical for the Gospel, too independent for a Redeemer; Abel bowed down before the majesty of Revelation. Cain's thoughts would be these: "I do not see what I have to do with my father's sin. I am told that the guilt of it is transmitted to me; but I do not believe in this kind of hereditary taint; and as for any personal sin, I do not see that anything which I have done deserves the penalty of death. I am not without becoming thoughts of God. I acknowledge His Being, I own His power, I adore His goodness. I am ready to bring my thank-offering to Him who blesses the labour of my hands, and causes the earth to yield her increase °; but as for any prescribed mode of worshipping Him, I must myself be the judge of its propriety and reasonableness; and as for acknowledging myself a sinner deserving of death, or offering a sacrifice which indicates this, and which is supposed to have reference

---

° "Caini *oblatio*, confessionem duntaxat obligationis habuit, Abelis *victima*, confessionem peccati, et desiderium expiationis."—*Bengel*.

to some future atonement, against this my reason rebels." And so he brings his offering, which testifies indeed to a Creator's bounty, but conveys no recognition of a Saviour's love. Far different from this is the mind of Abel. "I acknowledge," he would say, "my father's guilt and my own. But blessed be His name that He has provided a remedy. I will go into His presence, and take a sacrifice which shall be a token of my faith in the Victim that He will one day provide, and in return for His amazing love I will consecrate myself, with the best that I have, to be henceforth wholly His[p]." Thus while Cain, through his unbelief and neglect of the Divine warning, became the founder of the race of evil men, so did Abel, by his faith and obedience, take the foremost place amongst the citizens of the heavenly City. And he was a type of Christ, not only in his meek and blameless life, and in the nature of his offering, but also in his death; for as he was sacrificed through the envy of his brother Cain, so was Christ Jesus crucified through the malice and envy of His brethren the Jewish people. And as the great Shepherd of the sheep was brought again from the dead, so shall this primitive shepherd, and all the saints and martyrs who have followed his faith, be brought again by a glorious resurrection, through the power of that "blood of sprinkling, which speaketh better things than that of Abel."

Well, then, might the Apostle say of Abel that "he, being dead, yet speaketh." Eloquent, indeed, are his utterances, and full of instruction, as their echoes ring from his early tomb, and are repeated from age to age along the mighty reach of six thousand years. They tell us of the first conflict of Reason with Revelation,

[p] See Meditationes Hebraicae, *Rev. W. Tait*.

and of its inevitable issue. They tell us that our worship of God must be of faith as well as of reason. They tell us that if it be of faith, there will ever be mingled with it the acknowledgment of our sinfulness, and that therefore we must bring our sin-offering as well as our thank-offering to His footstool. And this we do by ever bearing in our hearts the remembrance of Christ dying for us, and by presenting Him by an act of faith as our trespass-offering to the Father. This we do especially in the Holy Communion, in which it should be our prayer that "the commemoration of the true Sacrifice may be well pleasing to God the Father, even as the gifts of Abel were accepted by Him[q]."

Then, further; as we place ourselves in thought by the grave of this early victim of violence and death, he speaks to us by his name. He tells us that "man is like to vanity, and that his time passeth away like a shadow." He tells us that we must expect to suffer for righteousness' sake; but he tells us also that this earthly life is not the highest boon. Eternity is our real lifetime, and death is but its birth. Who would exchange the brief life of Abel, taken quickly though violently to his everlasting reward, for the protracted and miserable existence of the murderer and fugitive, Cain? Not, indeed, that long life on earth is not to be desired. I know that out of life are the issues of eternity. Long life is therefore a blessing, if it be devoted to God; but if it is consumed in vanity or in sin, then I say, come early death, rather than an existence, the remembrance of which will sting hereafter like an adder. I know that there is not one in this congregation to-night who will deny that he was born for a nobler purpose than that of living to himself, and

---

[q] Ivo Carnotensis, quoted by J. Mede, p. 377.

for the gratifying of his passions. Every one of you must be conscious that he was born for something higher than this. You have been created, redeemed, and regenerated, that you should live to God's honour, and fulfil the great purposes of your existence ; and there is something noble and dignified in the thought that we are, all of us, servants of the great King, appointed to do His work. With such a view of life we may pronounce long life to be a blessing ; for then there is not a duty we perform, not a word we speak, not a thought we think, which may not add to the sum of our happiness in the future glories of the everlasting kingdom.

But we must think not only of ourselves but of others. Let me then, lastly, urge it upon you to seek so to live, that when you come to die you may deserve the epitaph of Abel, "He, being dead, yet speaketh." It is a pure and noble ambition to aim at handing on our names and examples with honour ; and this, God helping us, is within the reach of all. To live, so as to finish the work which He has given us to do ; to live, so as to please Him and to be useful to our brethren ; to regard time as a precious talent, not to be wasted in indolence and self-indulgence, still less to be sacrificed to criminal pursuits and sensual pleasures ; to regard time, I say, as a trust, and therefore not to be killed as an enemy, but to be redeemed as a friend ; to live, every day, so as to give a good account of every day; to be humble and self-denying, and earnest and true, and generous and pure ; to search out our faults and to try, honestly and manfully, to overcome them ; in one word, "to live by the faith of Him who loved us and gave Himself for us,"—the influence of such a life is undying. The seed thus sown shall become a tree, yielding fruit for those that shall come after, yea, stretching out its branches into eternity itself. And by such a life you, after death, shall yet speak,—speak as with a thousand tongues [r],—testifying to ages yet to come, that, whatever scornful and unbelieving men may say, Christianity is after all a great power in the world; and that the only religion which has any real abiding hold upon the hearts of men is the religion of the CRUCIFIED ONE.

[r] "Abelis olim occisi fides, innocentia, martyrium, et memoria adhuc recens est et celebratur apud omnes fideles, eosque ad sui imitationem exhortatur melius quam si Abel mille linguis eos exhortaretur."—*Cornelius à Lapide, in loc.*

SERMON IV.

Noah.

HEBREWS xi. 7.

"By faith Noah, being warned of God of things not seen as yet, moved with fear, prepared an ark to the saving of his house; by the which he condemned the world, and became heir of the righteousness which is by faith."

THE great servants of God, generally speaking, share in a common stock of thought, feelings, resolves, efforts, sacrifices, which lifts them, as a class, above the ordinary level of men, and makes them what they are. They live in the world, without being of it; they look beyond its narrow frontiers for their main interests and ruling motives; in some shape or other they give up what they see for what they do not see. They feel, and feel practically, that human life is at once blessed and awful; blessed in its opportunities, awful in its possibilities. They act as men who are in possession of the clue to its real meaning; they know and feel why they are here, and whither they are going. And thus, in communion with the Author and object of their existence, and in doing His will, so far as they know it, by themselves and among their fellow-creatures, they realize the true scope and dignity of their being, and they fertilize the lives of all around them. "Blessed is the man that hath not walked in the counsel of the ungodly, nor stood in the way of sinners, and hath not sat in the seat of the scornful.

But his delight is in the law of the Lord, and in His law will he exercise himself day and night. And he shall be like a tree planted by the rivers of waters, that shall bring forth his fruit in due season. His leaf also shall not wither, and look, whatsoever he doeth it shall prosper[a]."

But each among the servants of God has some distinguishing characteristic over and above those which are common to them as a body. As in nature no two flowers, no two animals, no two human countenances are exactly alike, so in grace this reflection among the creatures of the Creator's exhaustless resources is even more apparent. Each who has a part, still more, each who is eminent in the kingdom of grace, has in it a place, a form, a work, which belongs to no other; his character or his circumstances make him, at least in some respects, unlike any who have preceded or who follow him.

The great patriarchal figures who move before us in the sacred record of the antediluvian age are naturally shrouded in the dimness of a remote antiquity. Of the seven names which connect Seth with Noah, one only attracts a specific moral and religious interest: we pause at the holy life and the glorious translation of Enoch. With this exception there is little to arrest the attention beyond the length of years which was granted to those earliest generations of men. Strange, almost inconceivable, such longevity may perhaps appear when we contrast it with the existing limit of human life; but it is in harmony with the general scale of gigantic power to which all the most reliable evidence relating to the old world consistently points as characterizing it[b]. Life in that early age was com-

[a] Ps. i. 1—4.   [b] Delitzsch.

paratively simple, regular, free from the social mischiefs and the weakness which came with a more highly organized society. The climate, the weather, the natural conditions under which man found himself were probably different from those which succeeded the Deluge. And Paradise was still recent, so that, although its great prerogatives had been immediately forfeited, the endowments of which man had been originally possessed, such as immortality, would die out only gradually, and as if by a process of progressive exhaustion[e]. Thus it was that when Enoch was translated into eternal life with God, without passing through disease and death, five generations of ancestors must still have been living, Jared, Mahalaleel, Cainan, Enos, even Seth; while Enoch's son Methuselah, and his grandson Lamech, had already attained an age far beyond that of modern man; Lamech was 113 years old. Of that antediluvian line, at the date in question, only Adam had been taken to his rest; only Noah was not yet born.

Sixty-nine years elapsed between the translation of Enoch and the birth of Noah, and during that period the moral atmosphere of human history had very rapidly darkened. This result appears to have been due to two main causes beyond the constantly self-aggravating effects of the Fall. In the fourth and fifth chapters of Genesis the developement of the human race is traced through two entirely different lines,—that of Cain and that of Seth. It would seem that, notwithstanding the sense of the phrase elsewhere in Scripture, the Sethites, and not any beings of a higher world, are in this connection meant by the august title, "sons of God;" and the intermarriage between the Sethites, who had preserved the higher and better traditions of Eden, and

[e] Delitzsch.

the Cainites, who had entirely lost them, issued in the rapid moral degradation of the posterity of Seth. Distinct from this, but contemporaneous with it, was the appearance of the Nephilim, the "giants" of the English Bible. They seem to have been social tyrants rather than physically unnatural monsters; they made the law of might the ruling force of that primitive society. The corruption of the old world was therefore mainly traceable to two factors, each fatal to the moral well-being of man;—it was due to social oppression, or cruelty, accompanied by a reckless sensuality.

Lamech felt the evils of his time; all seemed to him to flow, as it did flow, from the sin which had been perpetrated and from the curse which had been pronounced in Eden. He felt the burden of his labour upon the soil, and when his son was born, we read a proof of the father's melancholy together with the prophetic presentiment of a brighter future in the name of the infant: "And he called his name Noah, saying, This same shall comfort us concerning our work and toil of our hands, because of the ground which the Lord hath cursed [d]."

Noah's personal piety is described by the same phrase as Enoch's: he "walked *with* God." This expression denotes even more than that which is used in a divine command to Abraham, and in Abraham's description of his own life [e]. Abraham was to "walk," and did "walk *before* God." Still more carefully should it be distinguished from "walking *after* God," a phrase by which Moses enjoins obedience to the law in one age, and Josiah renews it in another [f]. To walk after God is to lead a life of obedience to the commands given

---

[d] Gen. v. 20. [e] Ibid. xvii. 1; xxiv. 40.
[f] Deut. xiii. 4; 2 Kings xxiii. 3; 2 Chron. xxxiv. 31.

in the divine law; to walk before Him is to be constantly conscious of His overshadowing and searching Presence; but to walk with God is something higher and more blessed even than this; it is to be, as it were, constantly at His side, and in His confidence; it is to be admitted to close and intimate communion with Him as with a most cherished Friend; it is to be in spirit what the Apostles were in the flesh, when they shared, day by day, in the streets and lanes of Galilee, the Divine companionship of the Incarnate Son. Under the Gospel, it is St. John's "fellowship with the Father, and with His Son Jesus Christ;" it is the equivalent to St. Paul's "being quickened and made sit together in heavenly places in Christ Jesus." Once only besides does the phrase occur in the Old Testament, when the Prophet Malachi applies it, not to the conduct of the Israelites generally, but to that of the priests, who stood in a closer relation to God than the rest of the people, and could enter the Holy of Holies, and hold intercourse with the Presence Which was veiled from the public eye [g].

Noah's piety, then, was of an exceptionally lofty kind. He is said expressly to "have been a just man, and perfect in his generations," and in the midst of the general corruption he "found grace in the eyes of the Lord." Of this general temper, his thankfulness after his deliverance is a sample; in order to express it, he sacrifices some of the little store which he had saved from the general wreck; and a sentence in Ezekiel implies that he had especial power as an intercessor with God [h]. Yet his intercession is classed with that of Job and Daniel, and his thankfulness was in the form, as in the spirit of its manifestation, an anticipation, to

[g] Mal. ii. 3.   [h] Ezek. xiv. 14, 20.

cite no other instances, of that of Moses. Holy Scripture, with its wonted simplicity and truthfulness, describes his fall, in his old age, into an error; whether of inadvertence or of weakness. It does not generally place him above the level of other servants of God. We have, then, still to ask what it was wherein Noah's specific and typical excellence more particularly shewed itself? And this question is answered by the passage we are considering in the Epistle to the Hebrews. Omitting all else—and there is much—which the history of this great Patriarch suggests, it bids us observe that "by faith Noah, being warned of God of things not seen as yet, moved with fear, prepared an ark to the saving of his house; by which he condemned the world, and became heir of the righteousness which is by faith."

Indeed, it is to this period of the life of Noah that all the allusions to him in the New Testament, with the exception of that in St. Luke's genealogy of our Lord, refer. In the mind not only of St. Peter but of our Lord himself, "the days of Noah" were especially that most critical period of 120 years which preceded the Deluge[1]. It is possible that the social or political interest of his life may have been greater at earlier or at later periods; it is certain that the intensity of its moral interest centred in this.

In Noah's building the ark at the command of God there are three main points to be considered.

1. It implies, first of all, that he had an earnest conviction of the sanctity and greatness of moral truth; a conviction which, beyond any other, is the basis of the religious character. He was surrounded by populations which had broken altogether with the laws of God; impiety, impurity, lawlessness were the order of the day.

---
[1] St. Luke xvii. 26.

"Every imagination of the thoughts of man's heart was only evil continually;" the corruption was universal, internal, profound. To a great many men a surrounding atmosphere of moral evil would be destructive of the moral sight. Those of us who know anything of our own hearts must know this; how easily we get accustomed to the sight of what is wrong, how soon we feel complacency, or something like complacency, towards it; how it undermines our sense of its malignity, and makes us, if not its captives, yet almost its tolerant apologists. "Neither doth he abhor everything that is evil," is a severe and exceptional condemnation in the mouth of the Psalmist. But how widely is it applicable! It is not that evil, triumphant as in Babylon, crushes us into acquiescence: the remnant of the Canaanites that is in the land suffices for the corruption of Israel. There it is; and we take it for granted, in ourselves and in others. It is part of the actual sum of human life and activity, nay, it is a very large part. Within our own hearts, perhaps, it finds something like countenance and sympathy. What is the good, we say to ourselves, of always finding fault with the weather or with an epidemic? We may wish that things were otherwise, but we resign ourselves philosophically to take them as they are.

This acquiescence in evil as inevitable, involves something beyond it. It leads us to shut our eyes to what the deepest and truest of all human presentiments—apart from the revelation of God—points to as its certain consequence. It blinds us to the fact that evil is, must be, followed, at some time or other, in some way or other, by punishment. Could it be otherwise, God would not be God,—a necessarily and intrinsically Moral Being; could it be otherwise, the first and most earnest affirmation of a healthy conscience would be untrustworthy. And yet we may, by familiarity—tolerant, indolent, sympathetic familiarity—with evil, learn first to forget that evil leads to punishment, and next, not improbably, to deny it. It is inconceivable, we say, that a world-embracing mass of evil should be punished; its very universality is its safeguard and protection: it might be punished, if it were an exception; it must escape, simply as being the rule. This is what we tacitly say to ourselves: we shut our eyes to a first truth of morals, and we flatter ourselves that we are only recognising facts.

It was against this silent and fatal influence of a corrupt moral and social atmosphere that Noah's life was a protest and a resistance. Scripture says, he was "perfect in or among his generations," and those generations were altogether corrupt. He was a preacher of righteousness, when righteousness was at a discount and unpopular. He walked with God, when mankind at large had forgotten Him. He did not think the better of sin, of its real nature or of its future prospects, only because it was practised on a large scale, and with considerable apparent impunity. To Noah the eternal truths were more certain than the surface-appearances of life; he was certain that evil was evil, and that it could not but be followed by chastisement, because God is God.

2. Such a moral conviction, it must have been, which fitted Noah to listen to the Divine prediction of a coming deluge. God does not take the morally deaf and blind into His confidence. The words of Jesus Christ sound through all the ages of human history as the voice of a Divine Providence: "He that hath ears to ear, let him hear." He whose moral senses are alive, let him

listen to the proclamation of God's Truth; to others it will only be meaningless. "He that willeth to do the will of God shall know of the doctrine whether it be of God." Noah was "warned" of God "of things not seen as yet:" he was the subject in some way—we cannot determine in what way—of a supernatural communication. It may have been some sensible voice from without; it may have been an unmistakeably Divine assertion, yet from within. "God said unto Noah, The end of all flesh is come before Me; for the earth is filled with violence through them: and behold I will destroy them from the earth. Make thee an ark of gopher wood.... Behold I, even I, do bring a flood of waters upon the earth to destroy all flesh, wherein is the breath of life, from under heaven: and everything that is in the earth shall die.... But with thee will I establish my Covenant [k]."

Why should Noah believe this prediction sufficiently to act upon that command? Because God had spoken. That was his reason; that was his conviction. It was enough for him, he needed no more. But his conviction of the unchangeableness and truth of the moral laws of God would have rendered such an announcement, under the circumstances, to him at least *morally* intelligible. It mattered not that what was foretold was altogether unratified by any past experience. In the burning plains of Central Asia, the idea of an universal Deluge may well have seemed the wildest of imaginations; a thousand years, at least, of human history had already passed, and there had been nothing like it. Nature seemed to be unvarying in her movements: the sun rose and set, the seasons succeeded each other, the generations of living beings appeared and passed

[k] Gen. vi. 14—18.

away: there was a limited, and so to call it, a regulated variety, traversing this reign of a discernible and pervading order; but as yet there was nothing that met the senses to warrant the expectation of a vast and overwhelming shock or catastrophe. Why should it be otherwise hereafter? Why should this accumulated experience go for nothing? why should the sense of security which it so amply warranted be succeeded by apprehensions of a disaster to which, as yet, the annals of the world afforded no parallel?

The answer was, because God had spoken. Who that believes in a really living God can plead the observed invariability of nature against the declared Will of the Author of nature? After all, this invariability, so to call it, appeals rather to the imagination than to the reason. The imagination becomes so accustomed to it, so moulded by it, that it undergoes a certain distress at the thought of its violent interruption; but reason, true reason, is ever mindful of the limits which bound even her widest observations. Because we observe a continuing sequence of similar effects, it does not follow as a certainty, it is only a high presumption, strong in proportion to the range of our observation, that these effects will continue indefinitely. We are not really in possession of knowledge respecting any secret necessity rooted in the nature of things, which makes it certain that they must continue; and if we believe that the Mighty Author of nature is really alive, and that He is a moral Being, and not merely a Force, or an Intelligence; and that as a Moral Being He may have grave reasons for disturbing all this physical and social symmetry which encircles us, we shall not distrust Him if He tells us that He means to do so. So it was with Noah: he was moved with fear, with a reasonable and a religious fear. He did not treat the warning he had received as if it had been only an omen, appealing to his superstition: he "prepared an ark to the saving of his house."

The event in which Noah believed before it came was appealed to in a later age by St. Peter, as furnishing a reason for believing in a still future and greater catastrophe. St. Peter is writing at the very close of his life, and already a sufficient time had elapsed since the Ascension of our Lord to allow for the formation of doubts respecting His Second Coming, doubts which were based upon the seeming unchangeableness of the world and of the laws of life. "Where is the promise of His Coming, for since the fathers fell asleep all things continue as they were from the beginning of the Creation[l]?" The Apostle reminds those who argued thus that time has no meaning for the Eternal God, and that to apply our notions of the difference between greater and less portions of it to His Majestic Providences is to forget that there is simply no such thing as succession in His unbegun, unending Life. "Beloved, be not ignorant of this one thing, that one day is with the Lord as a thousand years, and a thousand years as one day[m]." But if Christ's delay meant nothing but His long-suffering, the unchanging order of the world could not be urged as a reason for disbelief in the catastrophe of a future judgment, because the past history of the world already contained at least one eminent example of such a catastrophe. "By the word of the Lord the heavens were of old, and the earth standing out of the water and in the water: whereby the world that then was, being overflowed with water, perished[n]." In other words, water

---

[l] 2 St. Peter iii. 4.   [m] Ibid. v. 8.   [n] Ibid. v. 5, 6.

had been the instrument by which the surface of the earth was moulded, and one of the constituent elements of its well-being and productiveness; yet at the creative word of God, from being a servant and a blessing, it became an overmastering force and scourge. What had been, might yet be; another element had yet a work to do in God's providence, and neither the lapse of years nor the regularity of the observed order of nature, were any real reasons for presuming that the final catastrophe would not come at last. "The heavens and the earth, which are now, by the same word are kept in store, reserved unto fire against the day of judgment and perdition of ungodly men[o]."

Nay, it is very possible that, with a larger knowledge than that which we at present possess, we might be able to extend the argument by additional illustrations. Some years ago it was usual to refer solely to the period of the Deluge the animal remains which have been discovered in caverns or beneath the surface of the earth. But more recent science urges that they imply a higher antiquity, and are found under circumstances for which no universal flood would sufficiently account. It may be so. Is there anything in the text of the Bible which obliges us to narrow down to six thousand years, or in any way to stint the measure of the world's antiquity, short of admitting its absolute eternity? On the contrary, between the record of the original creative act and the subsequent description of a gradual process by which, through successive periods,—"days" they are called,—the world was brought into its present state, there is room for a measureless interval or series of intervals. And if this be so, who shall say that many of the animal—it may be some of the 'human'

[o] 2 Pet. iii. 7.

—remains which are now pointed to as hostile or at least embarrassing to the Faith of Christians, are, after all, proofs and relics of some bygone catastrophes, of which, previous to the creation of the present order of things, this globe has been the scene, and by which ages of probation accorded to moral beings who have preceded us men, were, by the sentence of the Great Judge, violently closed? It is true that we are here altogether in the region of pure hypothesis; but, I submit that there is at least nothing in revelation which necessarily contradicts it; while, if it be true, it yields support to the argument of the Apostle, and it justifies the generous faith of the Patriarch.

Not that Noah's faith had anything to do with such cosmical speculations. Religious men may be glad to harmonize their convictions with the advancing but shifting and often inconsistent conclusions of human knowledge. But the foundation of their faith is one and invariable. They believe that He who made the world can control it: and when His purpose is clear to them, they do not allow themselves to lose sight of it only because their imaginations are powerfully impressed by the spectacle of a settled and common order of phenomena or institutions. They are therefore independent of scientific arguments, without being indifferent to them; they walk by faith and not by sight. They are quite certain that, whatever difficulties may be urged against His declared Will at the moment, God will in the long run justify Himself to man, and will vindicate the wisdom of those who in a day of trial and darkness have taken Him at His Word.

3. For a third point to be observed in Noah is his perseverance under difficulties. His faith was a practical principle, and it upheld him in the face of serious discouragements.

(a.) To begin with, he might easily have said to himself that there could be no real necessity for his personally exerting himself; that the threatened disaster would scarcely touch one who was already 480 years of age; that it would be enough to warn his children of what was coming when he himself would probably have entered upon his rest. Why should he rouse himself in advanced life to so great an effort as that which was required of him, instead of leaving it to be undertaken by younger hands? The answer in his conscience was, that God had said, not to others but to him: "Build thou an ark of gopher wood."

(β.) Again, he might naturally have dwelt upon the great mechanical and constructive difficulties of the undertaking. It is not to be supposed that these were left to be discovered for the first time by modern criticism. How could such an ark be built, so as to secure at once space and safety? How could it be provisioned, lighted, warmed? How would the several animals be gathered so as to enter it? how would it be possible to preserve them under conditions of weather and temperature so unlike their own? And then when would the scourge have passed? and how would it be possible to enter again upon the earth as a solitary colonist, amid the traces of so gigantic a desolation? Well may Noah's heart have sunk within him. Yet, he knew, God had said to him, "Build thou an ark of gopher wood," and he had only to obey.

(γ.) Once more. Noah had to begin his work, and to continue it, not merely without active support and sympathy, but under the eye of a public opinion, not so much hostile as contemptuously cynical. What was this extraordinary outlay of labour and skill? what was its purpose and meaning? how was it other than the crotchet of a visionary and a fanatic? Did he really think that his fancies would become true, and that the settled order of nature as well as the civilization and progress of human life were going to be buried beneath the flood which he dreamt of navigating? Was every one else wrong, while he was right? was his private information (if such it was) to be weighed against the collective experience and judgment of mankind? How they must have mocked at the entire undertaking! how naturally must they, in their aversion to the idea and object, have revenged themselves on the form and appearance! What airy criticisms must have been lavished on it in its earliest rudimentary shape, on each detail which was supplied to it, on its complete structure! what delicate and yet bitter comments on its uselessness, its ugliness, its utter opposition to the whole current of contemporary thought and feeling! How, too, some of the more liberal critics would have endeavoured, as if in scornful and condescending pity, to enter, although remotely and for a moment, into the strange hallucinations that could have produced it,—as if surveying from afar a mental curiosity, which only did not move their anger because it ministered so abundantly to their amusement! And then with what satisfaction and complacency would they have betaken themselves anew to the life against which it was a protest and a warning, as to that which was warranted by the common sense and judgment of the time, and by a force of custom and sentiment which, as the world grew older, was daily gathering new strength and empire. Our Lord has said that what took place then is an anticipation of what will be on the eve of the last Judgment: "As it was in the days of Noe, so shall it be in the days of the Son of Man. They did eat, they drank, they married and were given in marriage, until the day came that Noe entered into the ark, and the flood came and destroyed them all [p]."

Yes, there was a delay of 120 years, but the threatened judgment came at last. "The flood came and destroyed them all." Whether it was strictly universal or something less than universal; whether it covered Ararat without covering, for instance, the Himalayas; whether it can be explained by any combination of known causes or only by supernatural ones;—these are important questions, but they do not touch the moral interest of the narrative, they would only lead us away from it. The judgment came. It came to vindicate the morality and sovereignty of God; it came to justify Noah, and to condemn the generation which rejected him. It came to demonstrate the folly and emptiness of all the glitter and order of that ancient civilization; the irreverence and falsehood of that opinion which seemed at the time so well founded and so strong. There must have been a day,—an hour of uttered surprise, alarm, struggle, agony, despair,—when this was realized. Poets and painters have endeavoured to pourtray it. But as the mind dwells on any vast picture of human agony, the heart grows sick and the head giddy. In that buried multitude, no doubt, there were degrees of responsibility and guilt, known to and weighed by the Eternal Justice. The Apostle hints as much in a significant expression [q], which apparently implies that on the descent of our Lord's Human Soul into the place of the departed there was a compensatory preaching at least to some of the imprisoned spirits of the antediluvian world. But, the general result is a contrast between an overwhelming judgment and a signal mercy,

[p] St. Luke xvii. 26, 27.
[q] 1 St. Pet. iii. 19, 20, compared with 1 St. Pet. iv. 6.

—a judgment provoked by forgetfulness of the law and knowledge of God, and a mercy awarded to faith in His word, which was not sacrificed to false and narrow views of duty, or to baseless misgivings, or to the corrupt and corrupting opinion of the day.

What Noah's work really and mainly foreshadowed would have been obscure at the time; but we look back upon it from a vantage ground, which enables us to do it justice. Every Christian must see, in the labour and temporal salvation of Noah, the shadow of a greater Toil and a more complete Deliverance. Looking to Jesus Christ, humanity in its wretchedness and yet in its hope might use in a deeper sense the words of Lamech: "This Same shall comfort us concerning our work and toil of our hands." Like Noah, Jesus Christ was a preacher of Righteousness; He preached a higher and broader Righteousness than man knew before, but then, by His Passion and Death and gifts of grace, He robed man in it, and made His Revelation tolerable to human weakness by making its substance a gift to faith[r]. And as Noah built an ark for the saving of his house, so did our Lord build His Church to be the home of His followers, with the promise that against it "the gates of Hell should not finally prevail." His teaching, His example, His works of mercy and of grace, His bitter Passion and Death, His Resurrection from the tomb and ascent to Heaven, were all steps in this mighty work; the Divine Architect shed His very life-blood in the labour of construction. And at length Pentecost came, and the Eternal Spirit welded all into a consistent and enduring whole; and as the races and sexes and degrees of men passed within it at the heavenly call, lo! there was neither Greek nor Jew, neither

[r] Heb. xi. 1.

male nor female, circumcision nor uncircumcision, barbarian nor Scythian, bond nor free, but Christ was all and in all[a]. And although, since those earlier days, the passions and errors of men have raised walls of partition within the Divine Fabric over and above the 'stories' which He ordered to be made in it[b], yet these most assuredly will not always last; they are human, while the Ark itself is Divine. Even now it floats upon the waters, upon the vast ocean of human opinion and society, and we, without any merit of our own, but of His free grace and mercy, have been permitted to enter it. Over us was uttered the prayer that "the Everlasting God, Who of His Great Mercy did save Noah and His family in the Ark from perishing by water," would look upon, wash, and sanctify us; that being delivered from His wrath we might be "received into the Ark of Christ's Church, and being steadfast in faith, joyful through hope, and rooted in charity, might so pass through the waves of this troublesome world, that finally we might come to the land of Everlasting Life[c]." We may, of course, if we will, plunge again into the waters; but we have only ourselves to thank if the Ark of the true Noah does not land us at the last on the Mount of God.

It may be useful to insist upon one or two practical conclusions which are suggested to us by the life and work of Noah.

(a.) It suggests, first of all, a particular form of duty, which at certain times in the world's history may press very heavily on the conscience of public men whether in Church or State; and, at certain turns in life, upon all of us, however private and retired our place and work may be. I mean the duty which may arise upon

[a] Col. iii. 11; Gal. iii. 28. [b] Gen. vi. 16. [c] Baptismal Service.

our seeing, or believing that we see, more or less clearly into a future which has to be provided for, or provided against. Indeed, to endeavour to look forward and provide is a part of the work of those who are charged with the maintenance and support of large public interests. It is their business to observe the direction in which things are moving, the forces which are coming to the front, the combinations or separations of forces which may be fairly anticipated, the general result that will emerge from and succeed the state of things with which they are actually conversant. Here, as elsewhere, to seek knowledge is to learn, at any rate, something; and God teaches us through our natural powers of observation and reflection, as well as in other and higher ways. Here, as elsewhere, to pray to know enough to be able to do God's Will in our day and generation, is to be answered; and, it may be, to have to anticipate deliberately much to which we would willingly be blind. Such a habit of looking forward, if its motive be higher than a speculative curiosity, will not interfere with the duties of the present hour: nor will it militate against the general temper of trustful resignation, which, in those who see furthest and deepest, is ever ready to leave its hopes and fears in the Hands of God. In private and worldly concerns, such foresight is not often either undervalued or neglected. No man continues to invest his money in an undertaking recommended by an imposing Prospectus and Board of Directors, if beneath its fair promises and apparent prosperity he can clearly see at work the causes of coming bankruptcy. But where the interests of others are only or chiefly concerned, it being probable that the man himself will have passed from the scene before his anticipations are realized, it is possible for him to find himself in Noah's position thus far ;—that he guesses a danger, a catastrophe, which is hidden from the sight of his contemporaries, and which imposes on him the plain duty of preparing to meet it.

Then comes his trial. Will he bestir himself to obey the behests of his conviction, or will he indolently fold his hands and let things take their course ? Will he say to himself, "After all, this is no particular concern of mine; it is the concern of everybody. Why should I be compelled to put myself out of my way in a matter that interests hundreds of other people as much as it interests me ? Why should I be taxed, heavily taxed, on the score of my farsightedness, while others can go on easily and quietly, with a perfectly good conscience, only because they are too unobservant or too inert to see, or to try to see, beyond the next turn in the road ? I will let things take their course ; there is no necessity on my part for a chivalry which will be mocked at till it is justified by events, and which, even if events do justify it, will soon be forgotten."

Will he reason thus, or will he reflect that knowledge, insight, farsightedness, if they really exist and are felt to exist, constitute responsibility ; that, even if he would, a man who sees further and knows more than others cannot be as others, morally, and before God or before men; that together with knowledge there comes, to a certain extent, and within the area which it covers, a forfeiture of that particular species of liberty which is a moral right of ignorance? Will he reason thus, and act upon his reasoning ? My brethren, it is a critical question ; possibly for the generation, the country, the Church to which he belongs, but certainly and under any circumstances for himself.

Can anyone with a heart think without sorrow of

that King of France whose reign covers the greater part of the last century, and who spans the interval which connects the Court of the Great Monarch with the reign of the Bourbon who died upon the scaffold? Few things in history are more piteous than the contrast between a boyhood of much interest and promise and an advanced life of abject, systematized dissipation. Yet Louis XV. was not wanting in penetration; and the gay revelries of Versailles did not wholly blind or deafen him to sights and sounds which might have convinced a less observant ruler that the fountains of the great deep of national life were breaking up, and that a new order of things was imminent. Allowing for the difficulties of a traditional position such as his, may we not believe that an earnest and well-considered effort to improve the condition and assert the rights of the people, in the middle of the century, might have saved France from the torrents of blood in which the inevitable Revolution was baptized? Yet Louis XV. passed away, enervated morally and physically by pleasures which ministered only to the satisfaction of the hour, while the mutterings of the approaching storm were falling on his dying ear, and his last and deepest convictions became embodied in words which were too surely verified: "After us the deluge."

Nor can we walk the streets of Oxford, and know anything of the history of the buildings which meet our eyes, without encountering another illustration of the matter before us. During the two centuries which preceded the Reformation there were men in England who felt that a change of some kind was coming, and that it was their duty to prepare for it. They could not read history with our eyes; they could not look into the future as we look back upon the past; they knew not whether Reform or Revolution was before them. But at least, come what might, it could not but be well to gather and cultivate the highest learning of the time under the guidance and stimulus of Religion; and it was to this provident care of theirs that we owe the foundation of some of the noblest colleges in Oxford. It may be feared that the highest aim and desire of their great legacy will not be handed on to the generations that will follow us; and yet it may be the duty and privilege of our day, under other yet not altogether unlike circumstances, and on a humbler scale, to leave at least one modern institution in Oxford where human learning will still be blessed by Christ, when we of this century shall have gone to our account.

From the State and Education it is natural to pass to the Church. Nearly forty years have now elapsed since a few of the purest and loftiest spirits that ever breathed the air of this place saw in the suppression of some Irish Sees a warning to prepare for more serious emergencies. They, too, might have said, that as private clergymen and teachers they might well let things take their course, or leave the work of struggle and of protest to those who were set in the high places of the Church. But their insight into the future, such as it was, was their own; and they could not transfer to others the responsibility of possessing it. They knew that the real cause of present disaster, and the most serious menace of future danger, lay not in any exceptional irreligion on the part of the State, but in the fact that Churchmen were at best half-hearted in professing their Creed: Samson's locks had been shorn, and who could wonder that the Philistines were upon him. If the Church of England was to be loved and worked-for in the years to come, it must be by men who recognized in her something nobler than the plaything and creature of Parliaments and Statesmen, something more than one of many human organizations, designed to promote co-operation among believers in Christ. If she was not a Branch of Christ's Body, her sacred language was a studied unreality; if her Sacraments were not channels of Divine Grace, were not their administrators like the heathen augurs of old, who could not but smile as they passed each other in the Forum? These men understood that a Church, to be upheld, must be believed in; but they would have failed, and deservedly, if they had endeavoured to re-invigorate a faith which they themselves held to be untrue. In their belief that, whatever came of it, they must go forward, in their simple sincerity, lay the secret of their strength. Out of the old materials which were ready to their hands, they set themselves to build an ark of fresh and strong convictions; they laboured, by all the avenues to public thought and feeling that they could command, to persuade their contemporaries to mean the Creed which daily passed their lips, and to act upon it.

It may be true that that movement has been pushed to some unwarranted and lamentable consequences, that its original principle has been, in some cases, caricatured or perverted, that it has indirectly created some bewilderment and confusion. What is this but to say that its originators and conductors were human, and that they have enjoyed no guaranteed exemption from human liability to error? But look at it generously and as a whole,—look at it as its opponents, I venture to say, will look at it, when in the clear daylight of history it can be viewed without any disturbing rays of intervening passion; and it will, it must be said to have saved the Church of England from impending death, either by spiritual hysteria, or by spiritual atrophy. It has poured a tide of life,—the life of earnest conviction and of earnest work,—through all the arteries and veins of the Church of this land; and it is year by year adding to the spiritual force which alone can enable Christians to face the speculative or political anxieties of the future. He who exclaimed from Bagley, forty years ago,—

> "The flood is round thee, but thy towers as yet
> Are safe,"

at the sight of Oxford, foresaw clearly what was coming. And now that he is gone to his rest, it is not too much to say that he has done more perhaps than any in these last times to enable us of a younger generation to look forward to the rising flood, if not without fear on the score of our own possible disloyalty, yet certainly without misgiving as to the general and final issue to the Kingdom of Christ in England.

It is easy to exaggerate the importance of the age we live in; it is a subtle inclination of self-love which leads us to do so. Yet after allowing for this propensity or weakness, we can scarcely doubt that the present is a period of exceptional importance, whether to the State or to Religion, both in England and Europe. Scarcely a year passes without the crash of some old throne or constitution; and around us are taking place, silently but with astonishing rapidity, vast political and social changes, which cannot but lead to much besides in the years immediately to come. To be entering on the full powers of life in such days as these may be a privilege or a misery; as a man has or has not the heart to feel their moral solemnity. Alas! for those whose conduct at such a time exposes noble names and ancient institutions to a condemnation, which will make it at least difficult to link the past with the future. Alas! for those who can see clearly and far into that which is hidden from most of us, yet who enjoy their keensightedness, if not with a reckless levity, yet without feeling any generous desire to lend a hand towards making an Ark of safety for truth and goodness. For, on a great scale or a small, there will be, there is, some share in the work of Noah to be taken by all of us; and they who work most in silence and unobserved, may have at the last the largest share in the blessing of the great Patriarch.

And, leaving public interests and duties, there is one sense in which each one of us must build his Ark, and that quickly. To every man death is the Deluge, and life is the time given him wherein to prepare to meet it. If we would not sink beneath the waters, we must build our Ark; and we have much less than the 120 years of Noah in which to build it. What if this brief and precious period is passing from us while we stand aside, watching the efforts of others, either in moody indifference, or in scornful contempt! What if,—as St. Augustine said of some Christians in his day, whose natural energy furthered Christ's kingdom, while their hearts were not enlisted in His cause—our part is only that of the mercenary Cainites, whose services the Patriarch enlisted to build the Ark, into which, when the day of trouble came, they would not enter! Let us look into this matter, if it be for the first time, this Lent. Let us lose no more days in setting to work, and let us take heed how we set to work. The ark of Salvation, says St. Augustine again, must be built by the Christian out of the wood of Christ's Cross. We cannot ourselves furnish either the design or the material; but if God will not save us by ourselves, He certainly will not save us without ourselves, without our corresponding, that is to say, with His purposes of grace and mercy. Yet if He is with us, it matters little, although the clouds are sensibly darker than they were, and the fountains of the great deep are already breaking up. It matters little, though all be submerged before our eyes beneath the rising tide, if we know and are sure, upon the strength of His word, that after a brief voyage upon the waters, our feet will rest upon the Eternal Mountain, and we shall have our part in that mighty Thanksgiving which will never end.

SERMON V.
Eve.

GENESIS iii. 4, 5.

"And the serpent said unto the woman, Ye shall not surely die: for God doth know that in the day ye eat thereof, then your eyes shall be opened, and ye shall be as gods, knowing good and evil."

EVE's temptation and fall is the forerunner and counterpart of the falls of the sons and daughters of Eve, especially of those who are relatively in her condition, innocence as yet not sharply tried, the relative innocence of youth, before its first great fall. Her central temptation was, to seek against the Will of God, in a way of her own, forbidden by God, a good which God willed to give her in His way. So much is this an image of us, that a school has been found, which teaches, that Eve's act was a stage in human progress, "the first bold venture of reason, the first beginning of moral being, the happiest event of human history[a];" "the eternal myth of man, whereby he becomes man[b];" "the free-willed human spirit, bursting through the bands of instinct and the narrow home of animal peace, to soar unhindered to the hot struggle for hallowing[c]." "The narrator would shew, how man

---

[a] Schiller üb. d. erste Menschengesellschaft nach d. leitfaden Mosaisch. Urkunde-Werke, x. 389, ed. 1838, in Delitzsch *ad loc.*

[b] Hegel, Philos. d. Gesch., p. 333, ib.

[c] Einhorn (a Rabbi) Princip. d. Mosaismus, i. 65, ib.

found his way, out of moral ignorance and unindependence, and attained to moral knowledge and self-dependence, but therewith took on himself greater duties, than he had before to fulfil[d]." As if a debasing slavery to evil were a necessary condition of the knowledge of the difference of good and evil; as if previous estrangement from God were the essential preparation for being His friend; as if a ghastly independence of the All-wise were the necessary pathway to matured wisdom; as if the subjugation of our spirits to the natures which we have in common with the beasts which perish, were the indispensable stepping-stone and threshold to "the glorious liberty of the sons of God;" and disobedience to our Creator were essential to the perfection of beings created in His "image and likeness;" as if lawlessness were true liberty, wandering amid error the condition of the attainment of truth, abuse of our God-given faculties the essential practice of their use, unreason the handmaid of reason, moral darkness the one only vestibule to the true Light, the Light in which God dwells, the Light which He Is. But for sin, the Incarnation might have been without the horribleness of the Passion; we might have been as God, yea, God-united, engodded; and God might have been as one of us, without our being first as the Evil One or as the brutes; Heaven might have been without hell; the eternal Halleluiahs without those everlasting cursings and blasphemies; the reign of Divine love without that dark realm of hate; the ever self-unfolding communication of the satisfying fulness which God has and is, without that eternal impotent rejection of God which would that He were not.

But God willed, for our endless well-being, to be

[d] Knobel, *ad loc.*

loved with our full free-will. He would not (even if it does not involve a contradiction) be loved without our free choice. He willed to condescend to expose Himself (so to speak) to the free choice or contempt of His creatures. He empowered them, by His grace, to choose Him; He even made it a violence to their engraced nature, not to choose Him. But He subjected Himself to the vile indignity that He Who Alone Is, Who hath and is all Good, the perpetual Fountain of all Perfection as of being, should be rejected by us, who have no being save from Him, who have from Himself the power of rejecting Him, rather than not bestow on us the unspeakable dignity, freely to choose Him.

And so, since that ever-to-be-repeated choice is of such infinite moment, God gives us the history, not of the moving temptation only and the fall, but of the order of Satan's wiles and Eve's tampering with her tempter.

Satan prepares for the fall by exaggerating the prohibition. He would convey hard thoughts of God, without directly touching on the prohibition itself. "Can it then be," he asks, "that the Deity[e] (he omits the special name of God) hath forbidden you to eat of any[f] tree of the garden?" Much as he might say now, "Has the Deity forbidden all progress? Has He put bars to the intelligence which He has created, and fettered the free scope and use of the reason which He has made a created image of His own?" Or, "Does God indeed mean to forbid us the enjoyment of the appetites which He has given us?" As though to re-

---

[e] אלהים. The special name, by which God revealed Himself to man, יהוה, is omitted in this dialogue.

[f] The force of לא תאכלו מכל.

strain a mighty stream within a prescribed channel, that it waste not itself, and change not the fair bright face of nature around it into a foul morass, were to dam its course! Satan would not directly impinge on the commandment itself, as now, too, he never begins at once with suggesting the overt breach of some chief commandment. He knows well, "No one at once becomes all bad [g]." But he would familiarize the mind or lodge in it the thought, "the Deity *could* be hard." It was the beginning of the fall, to hold intercourse with one who had such thoughts, and had suggested them. The idea, although set aside as a fact, was lodged in the soul, which held parlance with him who had suggested it. Not to reject the first insinuation of evil, is virtually to consent to it. Eve's answer agrees in two ways with our wont, when giving way. It seems most likely that she added of her own to God's command. For in this state of original righteousness, the command "not" to "eat of the fruit of the tree," and "not" to "touch it," would alike be positive commands. Neither was wrong in itself, except in so far as it violated a command of God. Nature was whole *then*. There was no temptation to contravene it. Allegiance to its Creator was its only trial. When God forbids *us* to do anything, for fear that the first step should lead to the next, it is that the first is easier to *us*, is a less wound to conscience than the other. So the thought or imagination of sin, such as is forbidden in the "thou shalt not covet," lies nearer to us than the full violation of the seventh or eighth commandment. But in the state of man's innocency, when nature was not yet disordered, there was no stronger temptation to eat, than to touch what was forbidden. There was no occasion to place a fence

[g] "Nemo repente fuit turpissimus."

round a further law, when to break either would have been the same offence, the breach of a positive law of God. Had God forbidden to touch the fruit, to touch it had been the same offence as to eat it. Either, alike, would have been to do what God forbade. Eve's answer, then, fair as the words sound, betrays that Satan's poison had begun to work in her soul. She made out, that God had forbidden more than He had; the very suggestion which Satan had just more broadly made to her. "Of the trees in the garden we may eat, and of the fruit of the tree which is in the midst of the garden, God hath said, Ye shall not eat of it and ye shall not touch it." Then follows the other token of giving way. She adds, "Lest ye die." Not the sin itself, not the loyalty to her God, not the ingratitude in disobeying Him Who had so bountifully endowed her and surrounded her with all things fair and beautiful, not the thought of that daily converse with God, and His being with them as a Friend, not the dread of the severance of that relation of love with Infinite love, which God is, is foremost in her mind, but the penal consequences to themselves of the breach of the commandment, "Lest ye die." True, God had said, "In the day that thou eatest thereof, thou shalt die." True also that the dread of hell is often, in our now fallen nature, the first beginning of a conversion to God. True also, that, as it involves an eternal severance from, and loss of God, the fear of it may rightly quicken the converted soul in its exceeding dread of that which is the true severance from God, sin. But in our unfallen nature it was already a leaning to a fall, that the penal consequences of sin were put forward, rather than the offence against God. It is not, "My God hath forbidden it, therefore I cannot do it, and sin against Him

Who made me and daily continueth these peaceful blessings to me ;" but, "Ye shall not eat thereof, neither shall ye touch it, *lest ye die.*" She speaks of God as an austere Master, and forgets all His love.

Satan saw his advantage and seized it. Eve, thinking of the penalty to herself, not of her allegiance to her God, laid herself open to and invited the bold lie, "Ye shall assuredly not die." Nay, it was impossible that they should die. It was in contradiction with other certain truth, with the very name, which God Himself had given to the fruit, which He forbade, "the tree of the knowledge of good and evil." "For the Deity doth know, that in the day ye eat thereof, ye shall be as the Deity Himself, (i.e. thus far, in this point of knowing good and evil, which, Satan suggests, God had grudged His creature) "knowing good and evil." If, then, the knowledge of good and evil was to be the result of eating the fruit, then death could not anyhow be the immediate consequence of the act; else there would be no room or scope for those immediate effects, of which God spake by the very name. Yes, it could not be. There was a long future before them, a future, in which they should exchange their holy simplicity, or rather (as she would think) engraft upon it a knowledge, in its degree, like to that of God Himself Who forbade it, the knowledge of good and evil. But therewith he insinuated also that God withheld that knowledge, not in mercy but grudgingly. He Who made man in His likeness, willed not (Satan would have it) that he should be altogether like Him. He held back something, which would be good for His creature. Eve had lost sight of the thought of her allegiance and loving relation to God, in the thought of the penal consequences. The contradiction was plausible in itself so soon as it was out of her mind, *Who* had said it. It had, as have most of Satan's lies, a mixture of truth, which gave colour and gained entrance to the lie, which it disguised. So far they were to become like to God, that they should "know good and evil." But how? By losing their Divine likeness to God, Who had made them "very good," and united them to Himself by His grace; knowing evil, not, as He does, objectively, as something wholly alien from Himself and excluding Himself, but by *becoming* evil. Just as now Satan offers freedom by breaking God's law, and substitutes real slavery, the gradual weakening and almost destruction of free-will, the slavery to evil habits, for the glorious liberty of one-mindedness with God. Then followed the typical course of sin. She looked, she considered, she weighed, but the one side only, the side of temptation. "She saw that the tree was good for food and that it was a desire to the eyes, and a tree to be desired to make one wise, and she took of the fruit thereof and did eat." Holy Scripture probably veils the fiery consequences of that eating, and tells us only how Satan's promise was fulfilled. "Their eyes were opened, and" as the fruit of the tree of knowledge, "they knew" —what? "that they were naked." "They had become like God," but severed from Him. They knew good and evil. But instead of knowing evil afar, from the free height of good, they now know good only from the deep abyss of evil, wherein they had fallen. "Their eyes were opened." "Had they been blind before? They had been blind only to the mere sight of sense. They saw that they were naked and saw it not; for they saw themselves in God, saw all in Him, referred all to Him; nought of sense occupied their minds; in all they saw, they looked beyond to God; a mantle was over all, and that mantle was the glory of God[h]." The flesh was fallen away from the might of the spirit; the spirit from the life in God. Broken was the band between the spirit and God; broken the band of the spirit and the flesh. This alone remained, that, having lost that robe of original righteousness, with which God created them, they felt shame; that, having sinned against their conscience, they did no violence to the conscience which testified against their sin.

God has retained in us such likeness to Himself, even amid our self-made unlikeness, such traces of His image even amid our defacing of it, such secret unintelligent longing for Himself, even while we are wandering far from Him among His creatures, that, if we will not seek Himself, we must seek some perverted likeness of Himself. The soul must willingly or unwillingly own its Creator. If she turn from Him, she must still seek, without Him, what she findeth not pure or untainted, till she return to Him. "In her very sins she seeks but a sort of likeness to God, in a proud and perverted, and therefore slavish, freedom[i]." She could not, at first at least, be deceived but by "a false and shadowy beauty[k]." Pride, ambition, false tenderness, curiosity, sloth, prodigality, covetousness, anger, alien as they are from God, what seek they but to be as God? So S. Augustine traces out the deep thought. "Pride doth imitate exaltedness, whereas Thou Alone art God, exalted over all. Ambition, what seeks it, but honours and glory? whereas Thou Alone art to be honoured above all, and glorious for evermore.—The tendernesses of the wanton would fain be counted love; yet is nothing more tender than Thy charity, nor is

---

[b] Delitzsch, *ad loc.* [i] S. Aug. de Trin., xi. 8.
[k] Id. Conf., ii. n. 12.

ought loved more healthfully than *that*, Thy truth, bright and beautiful above all. Curiosity makes semblance of a desire of knowledge, whereas Thou supremely knowest all.—Yea, sloth would fain be at rest, but what stable rest besides the Lord? Luxury affects to be called plenty and abundance; but Thou art the Fulness and never-failing plenteousness of incorruptible pleasures. Prodigality presents a shadow of liberality; but Thou art the most overflowing Giver of all good. Covetousness would possess many things; and Thou possessest all things. Anger seeks revenge; who revenges more justly than Thou? Grief pines away for things lost, the delight of its desires, because it would have nothing taken away from it, as nothing can from Thee[1]."

Wonderful nobility and community with Himself, in which God created us! marvellous circumscription of our being by Him from Whom we evermore derive it, that even in sinning, rebelling against God, turning away from Him to His creatures, and turning them away from their rightful use, we yet cannot wholly emancipate ourselves from Him, we must seek some distorted likeness of Him, the more hideous, because it is distorted from so Infinite a Good.

But then look at the magnificent counterpart. Sin is an awful, in itself an irremediable, mistake. It is to miss our real, our only, our everlasting Good, for which our God in His love created us. It is to have taken a fiery draught which burns through all our veins, for "the rivers of pleasure at His Right Hand." It is to have taken our enemy for our god, slavery for freedom, a flickering meteor, an exhalation dancing around morasses, for the true light; it is to have lost for

---

[1] Id. Ib., n. 13. The original is fuller.

eternity that, for which God in His Infinite love created us. But then, if we have chased the ever-retreating shadow, the substance is there; if we have mistaken the glass for the pearl, the counterfeit for the royal image, the lie for the truth, still the counterfeit is the pledge to us of the existence of the glorious original; the forgery, of the true God-stamped image; Satan's lie, of God's truth. God, Who made us for Himself, made nothing in us, for which He provided not the full contentment; and that, not hereafter only, but now. Long we for freedom? He will make us "free indeed," He will give us freedom, which they who have it know to be real. Long we for knowledge? He has spread wide open for us the boundless variety of His creation, but above all, He gives us a real knowledge of Himself, He opens to us His own being and the mysteries of His love, where our only darkness is from the excess of His light. Long we for love? *Here*, too, pure love has an intensity of joy, an image of heaven; so that it has been truly said in a measure, that "love is heaven and heaven is love;" and we scarcely turn from sin to God, but He sends a thrill of love into the soul, the faintest touch of which is above all creation. And beyond,

"The heart that loveth knoweth well
What Jesus 'tis to love."

In many things (would God I could think it was still in all, my sons) ye must be in that first stage, in which your temptation is to a forbidden fruit, as yet untasted. In whatever degree it has not been, ye know that the first stage is to think that there can be anything good besides or against the expressed mind or will of God; the next is to question, "Can God indeed have meant to forbid this?" "Hath God indeed said?" Can God indeed have meant to lay such and such restrictions on His creature? To what end should He have placed the tree of knowledge in the midst of the garden, unless He meant us to eat thereof? The soul dares not at once openly rebel against the known will of God. If it *will* not be of the same mind with God, it must set itself to persuade itself that God is of the same mind with it. It is a necessity of our being, until we are lost, to be in harmony with Him Who is the end of our being, God. It is not all fear of punishment; still less, slavish fear. It is a holy dread to burst the band of union with God. Self-deceit is the soul's screen to hide from its eyes its severance from God. It dares not look its deed in the face, and do it. It snaps the bond of love, but looks away. The heathen persuaded themselves of old that the gods were the patrons of their sins. "Shall I not do, what the great Jove did? I did it gladly[m]." They consecrated their sins to their desecrating gods. The worst sins were, in nature-religions, the most consecrated. *They* said, "The gods meant this or that." In Christianity, men say more modestly, "Must not the God of nature have meant it?" After habituation to sin, the ἀκρατὴς becomes the ἀκόλαστος, and says boldly, "God did mean,"—what God in the most express terms forbade.

And so, as to faith. Hath God indeed said, that, on this very day Almighty God took our poor human flesh to be united co-eternally with His Godhead, and that, in the humility of the Virgin's womb? has God indeed said, that He Who, in our human time, was two days old, was Almighty God? or that God Himself, in our Flesh, was crucified? or has He indeed vouchsafed to

[m] Terence.

tell us how He Himself exists in His Co-eternal Love, Father, Son, and Holy Ghost ? Or has God indeed said, that He has set Himself as our free choice, freely by His grace to choose Him, or freely, despising His grace, to reject Him, to be (oh, misery of miseries !) eternally miserable by eternally rejecting *Him*, Whom the soul knows to be the end and centre of its being ? Indurated unbelief decrees peremptorily, "There is no god," or "human nature is god," or "we have no free-will or no immortality, but are like the beasts which perish." But unbelief ever begins, "Hath God indeed said ?" meaning, We cannot or will not think that He hath said it ; and quickly there follows that further thought, " He ought not to have said it, or so to have circumscribed the judgment of His creature."

Then follows, or is almost one with it, " Assuredly thou shalt not die." For God plainly cannot punish what He has not forbidden, or count it to be a rejection of His declared truth, to deny what His creatures have ruled for Him, that He cannot have meant to reveal. Only Almighty God and we are somehow to change places. We are to be His critics and judges, not He our Judge ; we are to rule for Him, what He shall reveal to us. We are (which it comes to) to make our God, instead of having as our God, Him before Whom the Seraphim with their burning love veil their faces, from Whom the highest Intelligences are content ever to receive something of His exhaustless Fulness ; Him, in whose tender love we reposed in our childhood ; Who never failed us ; Him Who made us ; and to depend on Whom was our peace, and the full contentment of our joy.

Such were the forerunners of the fall. Then followed the, alas ! so often-repeated history. " She saw," " she took," "she ate," "she gave to eat." She had got rid of the fear of God. Why should He, how could He, punish so disproportionably an act so slight? She had seen His bountifulness; she had not seen its withdrawal. The seducing spirit who spake with her had disobeyed and had not died. All other fruits in the garden had been harmless: the fruit of the tree of life had, by God's appointment, some mysterious influence for good; why should not the fruit of the tree of knowledge? She had not *our* experience, to which everything speaks of the death of the body; the sun shone on no new-made graves then; no parent's loss foretold the death of the child. She would "rather believe that God could forgive the sin," that He could threaten what He would not fulfil, "than endure not to know, what this thing was, which He had forbidden," or *why* He had forbidden to eat thereof. Satan cannot persuade *us*, against our daily experience of human mortality, that we shall not die the death of the body. But it is the self-same argument, by which he prepares our falls; "Ye shall not die eternally." God threatens "the worm which shall never perish," "the inextinguishable fire." God is disbelieved, His creature's lie is believed.

Secure, then, from harm (as she thought), *she saw.* She looked what it could be. Alas, if one were to name in one word, the parent of sin, the ante-dater of all other temptation, the destroyer of purity of soul, the corrupter of the senses, the disputer with God the Holy Ghost for the possession of His temple, the soul,— earlier, mightier than all passion but *that* which gives it its food and nourishment, and strengthens its mastery, it is,—ye know, my sons, what I mean—(Oh, how Satan repeats his hellish triumph over Eve, when he has awakened it)—Curiosity. Victory were, by God's grace, comparatively easy, were it not that the devil's porter[n], curiosity, opened the gates, and brought in those beasts of hell which lay waste the soul. They who have not, in boyhood, indulged curiosity are blessedly exempt from a whole embattled army of trials which it lets in on the poisoned soul. The baleful poison of the tree of knowledge has not spoiled the imagination, stirred up passions by nature happily asleep, created longings which belong not to its age, nor taken the will captive, when innocence would still start back from completed guilt.

> "Curiousness, first cause of all our ill,
> Is yet the plague which most torments us still."

Sins within the soul sometimes wound more gravely, are more perilous, can, in the nature of things, be more indefinitely multiplied than outward sins, though the outward sins of the same kind are seldom wanting. "Every man is tempted, being drawn forth and enticed by his own sin; then lust, having" by union with the will, "conceived, bringeth forth sin; but sin being perfected, bringeth forth death[o]."

Eve saw that the fruit had its threefold attractions. She had seen it before, but without the desire to eat; now she gazed outwardly at the lusciousness of its look, the invitingness of its beauty; and inwardly she saw all those tempting properties, of which the serpent had told her, the promised knowledge; and, gazing on these, she (as we have learned from her) forgot all besides. All other delights which God had spread so bountifully around her, the delights of every sense, when the senses, too, were pure, and everything of earth was transparent with the beauty of heaven; her innocent love for him,

[n] S. Thos. Aq. in Gen.   [o] James i. 14.

from whose being her own was derived; her immediate relation to God her Creator; her intercourse with God as a Friend—all was forgotten in that long, curious, empassioned gaze. "Why gazest thou," says S. Bernard[p], "so intently on thy death? Why cast thither so often thy straying eyes? Why love to gaze on what thou mayest not eat? Sayest thou, 'I stretch my gaze, not my hand; to see is not forbidden me, only to eat.' Fault though it be not, it is fault's index. For whilst thou art intent on one thing, the serpent secretly glides into thy heart, speaks blandly to thee, holds thy reason by his blandishments, thy fear by his lies, saying, 'Thou shalt in no wise die.' He augments thy anxiety, while he stimulates appetite; he sharpens curiosity, while he suggests cupidity; at length he offers what was prohibited, and robs of what was allowed; he offers an apple, and steals away paradise; thou drinkest deep the poison, thyself to perish and to be the mother of the perishing!"

"She ate and she gave to her husband with her, and he did eat." O horrible aggravation of sin, with its almost impossibility of perishing alone. Eve was emancipated from the yoke of the prohibition which she had never felt until she rebelled against it; she was proud of her liberty, her progress, her independence; she was all in all in herself; she had eaten and she had not died; no remonstrance of God pleaded against her, no sentence of God had condemned her, the echoes of the "in the day that thou eatest thereof, thou shalt surely die," had faded away. God's threatenings were not so real. Intoxicated with her impunity, with a whole wide future of successive triumphs before her, with proud hopes of her self-acquired likeness to God,

[p] De gradib. humilit., c. 10. n. 30, Opp. p. 578.

she sought to associate her husband in this her new career, the partner of that glorious course which she had opened to him. "He ate." The fall of humanity was completed; the robe of righteousness was gone; Adam had become her partner again, but in shame. Dreadful fascination of sin! It is a miracle of mercy if a sinner escape spreading the feverish infection of the leprosy of his sin.

Such is the oft-repeated history; such the sad wailing note of warning, floating down, but too often unheeded, from the closed gates of our lost paradise. "If thou wouldest avoid completed sin, flee from beginnings;" tamper not with it; let Christ's Cross, the seal on thy brow, fortify thee against imaginings; trust not thyself to rule for thyself, that God may not have meant what, as His Word is true, He has plainly said. Remember the closing words of God's revelation to man: "If any one shall take away from the sayings of the book of this prophecy, God shall take away his portion from the book of life [q]."

Such was the fall. In the mystery of to-day [r] is the restoration. "In very truth," says S. Augustine [s], "we, too, confess it, that had the Lord willed in such wise to become man, as not to be born of a woman, this had been easy to His Majesty. For as He could be born of a woman without the man, so could He be born, not even through a woman (as was Adam). But this He did, that in neither sex His creature man might despair. If being man, as He was to be, He had not been born of a woman, women might despair of themselves, remembering their first sin, that the first man

---

[q] Rev. xxii. 19.
[r] March 25, the Feast of the Annunciation of the B. V. M.
[s] Serm. ad pop. 51, n. 3, Opp. v. 284.

was deceived through a woman, and they might think that they had no hope whatever in Christ. He came then as man, but born of a woman, as though saying to them, 'That ye may know that the creature of God is not evil, but sinful pleasure perverted it; lo, I am born as Man, lo, I am born of a Woman. I do not then condemn the creature which I made, but the sins which I made not. Let each sex behold its glory, let each confess its iniquity, and each hope for salvation.' The poisoned draught was given by a woman to man for his deceiving; let salvation be given to man to drink through a woman for his salvation. Let woman compensate for the sin that, by her, man was deceived, through conceiving Christ. Thence also women first announced to the Apostles the risen God. The woman announced death to her husband in Paradise; women, too, announced to men salvation in the Church. The Apostles were to announce to the nations the Resurrection of Christ; women announced it to the Apostles."

And not only so, but as our Blessed Lord overcame for us, in fact and in ensample, the threefold temptation of Adam, the eating the forbidden fruit in the "command these stones that they become bread:" the vainglory, "Ye shall be as God," in the "cast thyself down;" the covetousness, "Knowing good and evil," in "the kingdoms of the earth and the glory of them;" so He vouchsafed to His Mother, at the vestibule of the Incarnation, to reverse the temptations and disobedience of Eve. The vainglory of Eve was reversed in the God-given humility of Mary, when she was willing, if such should be God's Will, to become the scorn of man; the disobedience of Eve by the obedience of Mary; the faithlessness of Eve by the faith of Mary. In the well-known words of the Father[1], "With a fit-

---

[1] S. Greg. Hom. 16. in Evang.

ness, Mary the Virgin is found obedient, saying, 'Behold Thy handmaid, O Lord, be it unto me according to Thy word;' but Eve was disobedient, for she obeyed not, while she was yet a Virgin. As she, becoming disobedient, became the cause of death both to herself and the whole human race, so also Mary, having the predestined Man, and being yet a Virgin, being obedient, became to herself and to the whole human race the cause of salvation. The knot of disobedience received the unloosing through the obedience of Mary; for what Eve, a virgin, bound by incredulity, that Mary, a virgin, unloosed by faith. Eve disbelieved through vainglory, longing to be as God, and lost her place in the creation; Mary, through humility, blindly believed God's Word by Gabriel, and was placed above all simply created beings, or all possible creations, in a nearness of love and glory which cannot be repeated in any other creation of God hereafter, cannot be imagined, as Theotokos, the Mother of God."

She was the Mother of our Redeemer, and so from her, as the fountain of His Human Birth, came all which He did, and was, and is to us. She, being the Mother of Him Who is our Life, became the Mother of Life; she was the Gate of Paradise, because she bore Him Who restored to us our lost Paradise; "the gate of Heaven," because He, born of her, "opened the kingdom of heaven to all believers;" she was "the all-undefiled Mother of holiness," because "the Holy One born of her was called the Son of God;" "the light-clad Mother of Light," because He who indwelt her and was born of her, was the true Light which lighteth every man that cometh into the world.

Such is the contrast, my sons, which this day suggests, of faith and faithlessness, of self-elation and humility, of receiving all things from God, or trying to wring them from Him: of dependence on God, or a would-be independence of Him. Eve willed to receive from Satan what God for the time gave in measure only, and sunk our race in depths which we see around us, which we feel, alas! in ourselves, the bondage of this death, and, although saved, is a by-word. Mary willed blindly to receive whatever God should give, whatever He should appoint. And where is she? What has been, cannot cease to be. She who was the Mother of God-Man here, must be His Mother still. Little were it to be Queen of Angels. *The* special bliss must be the special love of the human Mother and the Divine Son.

Men tell you much of the grandeur of progress, the glory of independence, the bursting of trammels, the laying aside of antiquated notions, the being lords over yourselves. God grant that ye may be lords over yourselves, by being subject to the Infinite. God give you to burst every trammel which binds you. For His service is perfect freedom. God give you true progress, progress in God to the Infinite Wisdom in God. It is not the question what ye shall seek, but from whom ye shall seek it, from him from whom Eve sought it, who can give you but a lying semblance of the Gifts of God, or from Him Who alone hath true Knowledge, true Wisdom, true Light, true Riches, true Love.

Choose really, truly, fixedly to whom you will belong, whom you will be, whom ye will have, and may He direct and fix your choice, Who will be the everlasting Portion and Joy of those who choose Him.

SERMON VI.

Joshua.

HEBREWS xii. 2.

"Looking unto Jesus, the Author and Finisher of our Faith."

ALL the teaching of God's Church throughout the whole world points to Christ. He is the theme, all other persons and things are the preachers. He is the centre, upon Him all lines of light and evidence converge. He is the melody, which every harmony of psalmist or prophet accompanies and sustains. He is the reality, whose shadow (cast over the past and coming ages) makes the types and symbols of eternal truth; and teaches mortals in their softened light what eye hath not seen nor ear heard of the hidden things of God. From the day that man was made, the revelation of Christ began. In His image was he formed, the body that he bears was fashioned after the model of the first-born of every creature. From His lips in the garden in the cool of the day man learnt the first lessons of truth. From the tree that was Christ's symbol, by daily feeding on that sacrament of life, man's deathless being was renewed, and we can well believe that, had he remained faithful and unfallen to the end, Christ, as his companion and his friend, would have trained him on unto perfection; preparing for a crown without the sorrows of a cross; and translating to heaven the being so sublimed and purified, without the need of passing through the shadow of the grave.

But sin came, and these dreams of bliss melted away before it; and from ruined man, but for the enduring love of Christ, all hope of heaven was gone. Life forfeited, innocence lost, the image of his Maker broken and defiled; no more walking with God in the garden, no more eagerness of conscious purity to meet the eternal eye, no more gathered food of life beneath that sacramental tree. Paradise lost, and peace, which is man's perpetual paradise, lost too. Stript of the seamless robe of innocence, which they had hitherto worn in their unconscious nakedness; and clothed in the skins of beasts that proclaimed that nakedness to all; the first parents of mankind went forth upon an accursed world to learn in labour and sorrow the lesson they had neglected in gladness; that one solemn lesson of truth, to learn which life is given, the lesson of obedience. To the paradise of their primal years they were to return no more. Sorer and heavier duties were henceforth to be essayed than the tilling and dressing of a weedless, thornless garden. Greater trials of faith than the passing by untouched one tree amid thousands rivalling it in fruitfulness and beauty. But when the discipline, which their passage through the world would bring, had done its bidding; when "the lust of the flesh" had been purged out in mortification and penitence, and prayer; and "the lust of the eye" in sorrow, and self-abasement, and self-sacrifice; and "the pride of life" amid the ruins of all human hope and joy:—then, again clothed in the raiment of light lost at the fall; and again conscious of an indwelling purity which would let them once more see their God; and again hungering and thirsting for righteousness, instead of for the meat that perisheth; they shall enter in at the gate of the city, and eat again of the tree of life which is in the midst of the paradise of God. And all the Church's teachings and trainings are to prepare for this. To seek out God's children in the midst of this naughty world, and wait by them, and watch over them, and cling to them, until they are saved for Christ; until His death has broken their hearts, and His life bound them up again; until patience has had its perfect work; until the old man with his deeds be put off, and the new man put on, which is renewed in knowledge after the image of Him that created him; until Christ be all, and in all.

This has been, since the day in which the first promise of His coming was made, the mission of His Church; and here and there through the long dark ages that followed the fall, light after light rose on the world in the persons of God's holy people. Lights, which, like the morning stars, lighten with their borrowed beams the darkness of the sleeping nations, reflecting on the earth a glory which they receive direct, but which has not yet risen upon man.

The first Adam, the figure of Him who was to come, the shadow of the Second; Eve, the mother of all living, her type who was to be "the mother of Jesus," as well as her type also, who, as the Bride of Christ, was to rear "brother and sister and mother" for Him; Abel, the offerer of a better sacrifice, "who being dead yet speaketh," pointing "to Jesus, the Mediator of the new covenant, and to the blood of sprinkling, that speaketh better things" than his own could do; Noah, "who being warned of God of things not seen as yet, moved with fear, prepared an ark to the saving of his house;" the great type of Him in whom alone is safety, when the wrath of God cometh on the children of disobedience; Melchizedek, "the king of peace, and priest of the most high God," who "without father, without mother, without descent, having neither beginning of days, nor end of life, but, made like unto the Son of God, abideth a priest continually," mysterious shadow of Him who, a high-priest for ever after that wondrous order, was to do for the faithful what for the father of the faithful was done of old, feed them under the symbols of bread and wine with His own most precious Body and Blood:—These, up to the time of Abraham, kept before the eyes of the believing amongst men the promise of salvation in Christ. They stood out from the felt darkness of the surrounding world. They uttered great truths, prolonging, each through a life, their utterance, that the echoes of what they taught might sound through all ages, go out into all lands, and their words unto the ends of the world, everywhere preaching Jesus; His humanity in Adam, His Church in Eve, His sacrifice in Abel, His redemption in Noah, His priesthood in Melchizedek; the new man, the child of God, the life and death of faith, safety in Jesus, and life in the communion that ever lives on Him:—these the great truths of the Gospel of Christ, which lives more than lips proclaimed; which, before the written word, were spoken out through man to man; and written with the finger of God on the fleshly tables of the heart.

But from the day in which Abraham was called, a more separate and clearly defined line was drawn round the Church of God. Called out of the world to be His witness, she must henceforth walk apart from its uncleanness, keeping herself unspotted, for the work her God had given her to do. She has a promise to hold, a written word to keep, a sacrifice to point to, a people to sanctify. To her the covenant is renewed, and the seal of Christ's suffering stamped upon it. Blood is shed upon the threshold over which each soul enters the Church of the living God. She is henceforth to be in the world, but not of the world, and to watch and wait for the coming of her Lord. She is to be made, in her future life, from its beginning to its close, a great lesson to man, a parable under which he may read all God's dealings with His people. She goes into bondage, that we may know the slavery of sin ; and is brought out of it with a mighty hand and stretched-out arm, that we may know the blessing of salvation in Jesus. She is baptized in the sea, to figure to us thereby Holy Baptism ; and in the pillar of cloud and fire she preaches the Presence of God.

In the wilderness, her wanderings and waywardness, her murmurings and rebellions, so often forgiven, and so often returned to again, teach us lessons of our own heart corruptions, which, looking so ungrateful as they do in others, may haply make us disgusted with ourselves, and turn our horror and our confusion in upon our own ungodly souls : and yet, through all those wanderings and waywardnesses, how wondrously were her children preserved. "They did all eat the same spiritual meat: they did all drink the same spiritual drink ; for they drank of that spiritual rock that followed them ; and that rock was Christ." And though with many of them God was not well-pleased, so that they were overthrown in the wilderness, still His covenant with His Church was unbroken and sure, and Israel was saved. The law had proclaimed its terrors and done its work ; had lifted up its standard, but could not lift the life of man to it; had shewn what was wrong, but had failed to lead to what was right; had terrified, but had not drawn. But what the law could not do in that it was weak through the flesh, God, sending His own Son in the likeness of sinful flesh, did for man. What Moses could not, Joshua did do. He became the Finisher of their faith, who, under his guidance, entered into the promised land. And that which He who is "the author as well as finisher of our faith," does in and by Himself for His Church, and every individual member of His communion, from the first to the last, from the font to the grave, Joshua, but a part of the great symbolic whole, did for that symbolic Church, which had so long worshipped in the wilderness. It took generations to tell out the one story, to perfect the one work of which Jesus is the author as well as finisher for men. Abraham, the father of the faithful, the giver of his only son: Isaac, the child of promise, the willing victim: Joseph, the betrayed and sold by his brethren, yet in the day of death the "Saviour of all men, specially of them that believe:" Moses, the deliverer, the lawgiver, the mediator, the comforter, the guide, the friend: Aaron, the high-priest, entered within the veil, touched with the feeling of our infirmities, tempted as we are: and lastly, Joshua, the saviour, the captain of Israel's salvation; not the author, but the finisher of the great work of faith which God had appointed them to do.

These all, each a part of the great whole which stretched over ages, wrought out, each in his appointed time and way, the salvation of God's Church on earth; and brought the children into the fulness of the promise made unto their fathers.

All helped toward their salvation, but to the last the

name of Saviour seemed more naturally to belong. Oshea, or Saviour as named from his birth; Jah Oshea, or the God-Saviour, as named anew by Moses, in the spirit of prophecy; every feature of his life and office typified the great Jah Oshea, or Jesus, the Saviour of the world. In bondage with his brethren, suffering with them, side by side, in all their wanderings and woes, bearing the yoke in his youth, the purest and most perfect of men recorded in Scripture. He who went to spy out and prepare a place for them, and came back to take them himself to that place: the bearer of grapes from Eshcol, whose wine they would one day drink new in their Father's kingdom. He to whom the law, as a schoolmaster, led; who did what it could not do; whose office on the banks of Jordan began, ere he entered into warfare for his people; who honoured not himself, but his great Master, whose work he had been commissioned to do; fulfilling to every tittle the whole law, and holding up that to men as their only rule and standard. He went down into the grave of the waters, and led up his people out of them with a glorious resurrection. His twelve memorial stones, his Apostles to generations unborn. The driver out of the enemies of the Lord, the saviour of publicans and harlots, the gentle heart-searching judge, the purifier of sin from his people, the divider of many mansions, the renewer of covenants forgotten, the bestower of the blessing of peace. There is not a phase or feature of his character which does not, as the light of revelation falls upon it, shew forth Jesus.

And it is from him, and his work amongst his people, that we are this evening to endeavour to learn a lesson of truth. We, who are many of us still in the wilderness, unable to enter into the promised land because of unbelief.

That promised land is not heaven above only, but heaven also below. It lies not all on the other side of Jordan, (if, indeed, Jordan mean that "Death's dark stream," of which the poet sings,) a portion of it is on this side of the cold river, a foretaste of the rest which is beyond. And into it we should all enter before this mortal puts on immortality. We should not be waiting for heaven till we die, but living in heaven while we live. "For we which have believed do enter into rest," that "rest which remaineth for the people of God."

But having once, by this portion of the metaphor, brought out this truth which I would desire earnestly to press upon all hearts, I purpose not to pursue the symbol too closely, knowing how hard it is to make any metaphor work out in all things accurate and true; and longing rather for the one great object I have set before me, to make Jordan mean those waters of penitence through which men must pass, who have lost in the wilderness of sin the purity of their baptismal covenant; the cleansing which the passage of the Red Sea brought them from Egypt's defilements; and who must, through the deep waters of tribulation, enter into the kingdom of heaven.

Then our thoughts would pass on naturally from repentance to progress in divine things, renewal of divine life, triumph over spiritual enemies, entering into rest and peace, and all that blessed consciousness of being saved—not *to be* saved,—which is the too often lifelong unused privilege of the Christian.

To this, our Joshua, our Jesus, the great Captain of our salvation, alone can bring us. But if we range ourselves under His banner, He is pledged to bring us in safe. Yet not without some cost and toil and travail as borne by us.

Not without their implicit obedience did Joshua

bring in Israel. They had to "go forward" when the waters were at their highest, and believe, that the passage might be free. They had to cast away the filth of the flesh, and get back into covenant with God, as the first evidence of their repentance; and though their wounded bodies made them an easy prey to the sword of the enemy, they had to trust Him who can keep the body safe when the soul leans on Him. They had to gather in strength in the Holy Communion of the Passover, before they could dare to face their enemies, and to cherish their hope of what in Canaan God *would* do, by their memory of what in Egypt He *had* done. Before the walls of Jericho they had to be as unarmed, though they were all well armed, men; and shewing themselves as nothing,—a voice only crying in the wilderness,—thus to magnify the more His name and power, whose word laid those walls in the dust. They had to learn in the discomfiture of Ai, what secret sin does to paralyse the powers of the Christian; and in the awful death of the sinner, the perfect holiness of God. In the one altar reared at Shiloh for their common worship, they were to learn the unity of faith which was to bind them all to one God, in one sacred rite; and in the alarm raised by the other altar, built through imprudent and too independent zeal, with honest purpose, but with great danger of sin, they were to learn that good intentions are not enough, when God's will may be consulted and known. In the share which those on this side Jordan took with those on that side, in the conquest of the land, they were to learn and to teach the link of love which binds together the one family in heaven and earth in one great community of interest; how they who have crossed the river still need the sympathy of those who wait on this side, and how our spiritual warfare on earth hastens the time when the souls that under the altar now cry "How long, O Lord, faithful and true?"—shall pass into the blessedness of heaven. And lastly, in that solemn renewal of their covenant with God under the oak of Shechem, where to Abraham of old the promise of the land had been renewed, and by Jacob on his return from exile, the strange gods and idol snares which had clung to some of his family, were buried out of sight; they taught the Church of Christ in all ages, that a covenant has two parts, duties to perform, as well as privileges to enjoy, and if the peace would be kept which God has given, it must be kept by His people's obedience.

These are our lessons to learn; God teach them to us in truthfulness and love.

So, then, turning altogether in upon our own hearts, and thinking only of our own spiritual condition, let us, by the light which the past has let into our souls, judge ourselves.

Where are we? in the wilderness, unmindful of our vows? looking back on the flesh-pots of Egypt? aimless, and restless, and unsatisfied, tossing to and fro in a hopeless purposeless life?

Or are we—turning to our Jah Oshea, our Jesus, and lifting up our eyes unto the hills whence cometh our help—preparing with earnest heart and full purpose of love to follow Him? To follow wherever He may lead? Through deep waters, if need be,—through pain and suffering and self-denial,—through whatever He may appoint as the fire which is to purify, as the water which is to cleanse? Or have those deep waters of penitence been past already through,—during this now nearly ended Lenten season? and have we risen up out of them on the other side, our feet standing on the very borders of the land of peace?

Or have we gone on unto perfection, putting down Satan under our feet, subduing our enemies under us? the passion of our penitence past, the high walls of our pride level in the dust, the accursed thing wholly put away, no peril to the Lord's host through our hidden disobedience? but the land of promise our own, with its richness, its abundance, its beauty? its corn and vintage, its milk and honey, its upper and its nether springs, its altar in Shiloh our rest? its peace in *the Shiloh* our God? "Knowing in all our hearts and in all our souls, that not one thing hath failed of all the good things which the Lord our God spake concerning us; all are come to pass unto us, not one thing hath failed thereof."

Is this indeed our portion? or do men when they hear it spoken of, look up in wonder, as if it were far beyond our reach on earth, and only to be found amid the everlasting hills of heaven? Do they dream of it as a possible future, when the hindrances of mortality are gone, when the Cherubim (their flaming swords quenched in the deep springs of eternal love—the blood of a crucified Redeemer,) drop them in the homage of a royal salute, to let the Redeemed, with their Redeemer, enter into the gates of a paradise closed against them so long?

Then, and then only, do they imagine that the peace, the perfect peace, in which he is kept whose mind is stayed on his God, the peace which passeth all understanding, of which they had heard so often, but never yet had felt it, do they imagine that this is to be found only in heaven, and is no necessary part of the heritage of Christ's people upon earth?

Alas! alas! what dishonour we do to the love, and the truth, and the power, and the glory of our covenant God!

Hath He not said? and can He not do it? Hath He not promised? and will He not make it good?

Where is your faith? the faith that could remove mountains as well as lay low walls? that could fill up seas, as easily as dry up rivers? Where is that substance of things hoped for, on which here we may lean, that evidence of things not seen, on which, more than our senses, we should rely? Where is that rest in Jesus, in which we are saved? that calm, quiet confidence which is our strength? that sweet perpetual song of heavenly devotion,—"My beloved is mine and I am His: He feedeth among the lilies,"—which cheers the heart and makes glad sunshine in the soul, "until the day break, and the shadows flee away?" Where are all these gracious evidences of the life of Christ within? If we want them, it is not through His fault, He is not less able to be a captain of salvation to us, than He was to make Joshua a captain of salvation to His people of old.

The sensible things of earth are not the only real things—nay, they are not, truly speaking, real things at all. All that story of Joshua and Israel (though a perfectly true story of a true people who won a true land), is still nevertheless but the shadow of things a thousand-fold more true. The conqueror and his myriads are dead, the land they conquered is deserted, in the pages of history only we now find the traces of what was done. But the true land is rich, and fadeless, and beautiful as ever, and the true Conqueror, "the same yesterday, to-day, and for ever," is by our side. We may enter in, and ever remain in the peaceable possession of our inheritance, whose riches and whose verdure can never perish, for they are as enduring as the everlasting hills from whence they come.

O if unhappily it should still be that we know not as yet that we are saved in Jesus, let us rest not until we are found in Him; found in Him without spot and blameless. He is the Author, let us rest not until we know Him to be the *Finisher* of our faith. The Alpha! why not the Omega? The beginning! why not the end? The first! why not the last? The all in all! able to save to the uttermost all who come to God through Him.

"Look unto Him, then, all ye ends of the earth, and be ye saved." Look unto Him through those days of darkness whose shadow will be over us so soon. Look unto Him on that accursed tree on which He died, that it might be the tree of life for man. Look unto Him as rising from the grave He tramples death under His feet. Look unto Him as, ascended up on high, He asks for grace to guide, and promises to come again, and crown that grace with glory. Look unto Him, as standing at the doors of your hearts, and knocking, and asking you to open and let Him in that He may dwell for ever there. Look unto Him, as looking even now on you, as He once turned and looked upon Peter, that by the moving passion of His tender love He may melt the sinner into tears. Look unto Him, and be saved by that very look of love, and enter into the rest of the redeemed. "Looking diligently lest any man fail of the grace of God." "Looking for the mercy of our Lord Jesus Christ." "Looking for and hasting unto the coming of the day of God." "Looking for that blessed hope, and the glorious appearing of the great God, and our Saviour Jesus Christ." "Looking unto Jesus, the *Author* and *Finisher* of our faith."

Rest not contented with a religion of dreams and wishes, of sighs and longings, of sickly hopes and fears. Take not as your motto the melancholy experience of the poet, who though he may have drank deeply of the nether, had never tasted of the upper springs, or else he could not have left behind him this sad proof of his unsatisfied longings :—

"Man never is, but always to be blest."

"We which have believed *do* enter into rest." "My blessing *is* upon My people." "Thou *hast* given him his heart's desire, and *hast* not withholden the request of his lips." "Thou prevent*est* him with the blessing of goodness." "Thou sett*est* a crown of pure gold upon his head."

Pass on into the present possession of these gifts of the Spirit. Pass on into the enjoyment of that good land and large, which the Lord hath given unto you; that land, in which *their* days shall be long, who in a life of obedience and duty claim the gift which waits on those who keep the first commandment with promise. For "he asked life of Thee and Thou gavest him a long life, even for ever and ever."

Lose not, through your own want of faith, one moment of that heaven below, much of which lies on this side Jordan ; into which we may pass through the gate of life, long before the gate of death hath opened to receive us. Then when the end comes to the struggle and warfare of earth, and down into the valley of the shadow (but remember only the *shadow*) of death, we shall go ; then the consciousness of the presence of peace will never pass away. And that awful change, through fear of which thousands upon thousands of God's redeemed and sanctified are all their lifetime subject to bondage, will be found to be only the opening of a cage to let the prisoned bird go free, and pass up into that glorious privacy of light which veils the invisible God. The unfolding of a door, whose shadow is only on this side, and that for the simple reason that sunshine is for ever on the other. The closing of the eyes in sleep after a busy and toilsome day, to open them on the freshness of a morning whose sun shall no more go down. The passing into the peace of Paradise.

Unto which may God vouchsafe to bring us all in His infinite mercy.

SERMON VII.

Belief in a Living God essential to the True Life of Man.

PSALM xlii. 2.

"My soul is athirst for God, yea, even for the living God: when shall I come to appear before the presence of God?"

BY whom this expression of passionate longing for the presence of God was first uttered, I will not now enquire. It was by the Holy Spirit that the words were taught, whether to David himself, or (as seems more probable) to ministers of the sanctuary in a later age. The forty-second and forty-third Psalms are the language of men who have lost what was dearer to them than anything in the world besides, and who cannot content themselves with new employments and another kind of life. Banished from home, they look back to their native hills; and as they look, their eyes are filled with tears. But chiefly they remember the glad solemnities which they kept in happier times, when they went to the house of God, with the voice of joy and praise, with the multitude that kept holyday; and, as they remember these things, their souls are vexed, their hearts disquieted within. Yet there is hope: this disquiet must not be suffered to possess the servants of God. He will yet send out His light and His truth, and bring them to His holy hill: they will go to the altar of God, the God of their joy and gladness, yet again.

Need I say that these Psalms have ministered to the longings of Christian hearts, too, in every age of the Church of Christ? Strangers in a foreign land, we long for our true home. We cannot be satisfied in our banishment. We do not see the God of our joy and gladness as we desire to see Him. He is present to us, indeed, sometimes, and for a while we have found delight in His presence. Then came a darker time; the sky was overcast with clouds: we prayed for light and truth that seemed wholly to have been lost. Even at the best, we have not that full communion with God, which we believe to be our true comfort and joy. We long to know Him better: we are tired of the world, and its heartless mockery, while they say daily unto us, "Where is now thy God?" He is about our path and about our bed, we could reply; but we want a deeper consciousness of His nearness. Hope soars above these poor experiences of ours: we will yet give him richer thanks, who is "the health of our countenance, and our God."

It may be said, indeed, that thoughts and feelings such as these are satisfied by material things. The look of the old church in which we worshipped long ago, the familiar chime of the bells we have heard in youthful days, the storied windows at which we have so often gazed with childish curiosity,—these things supply the comfort for which the exile longs. Give him these consolations, men say, and his craving will be set at rest. It is a mere sentiment, we are told, a fancy to be expressed by the poet's or the painter's art,—not a reasonable desire approved by the sober judgment of wise men, which thus thirsts and craves after sacred scenes and holy things. So say this world's critics; and there is some truth, of course, in what they say. I do not deny that love of art, and refined taste, and fondness for antiquity, nay, that superstition herself, may breed a craving in the heart for the objects on which it has been taught to dwell. Some men are the slaves of these feelings and tastes, and men not always the worst or most foolish of their race. Among the less cultivated, again, we know how easy it is for strong affection to lay hold of the most trifling, or the most grotesque, of the circumstances connected with a sacred name. The æsthetics, as the phrase is, of religion do constitute some part of its influence, do sometimes thrust themselves into its place.

But why is it, we must still ask, that these tastes and feelings, these longings and affections, so persistently wear the garb of religion, so constantly speak its language and adopt its style? You know what answer to give. It is because there does exist, deeper than these fancies and accidental feelings, that which corresponds to a real craving of man's heart, which he cannot but acknowledge to himself as true,—which he tries in vain, if he is so unhappy as to try at all, to reason away. The poor orphan child, who has never known a father's love, has something in him which yearns after it, and would embrace it, if only he could be so blessed as to enjoy it. And shall the children of our Father in heaven have no capacity for loving Him? Is it conceivable that He created them to be ignorant of their Maker, with no inward witness to His existence, and to His claim upon them for filial love? Easier it were to think with the infidel that man had been the offspring of some blind fate, some unintelligible necessity, than to believe him to have been the work of a Divine Creator, yet destitute of the power to love that Creator, and the wish to know Him in truth.

What shall we say, then? that, gifted with the power, burning with this desire, man may still be satisfied to live in ignorance of God? This, surely, is the strangest conceit of all. We are bidden to cherish what is called the religious sentiment: it is a valuable influence; it will elevate and refine those who yield to it; but it is to centre in itself. Our philosophical instructors, in their wisdom, desire to give us all the benefit of it; they are sensible of its advantages; they have observed that, without it, human society is apt to degenerate: for the mass of mankind, at all events, whatever they may say as to their own condition, religion of some sort is a necessity of life. Only it must never go beyond the domain of sentiment: they will not tolerate it when it appears in the character of faith. They bid us enjoy its consolations, and please ourselves with its hopes: we may have tender thoughts, pious meditations; the religious enthusiast may be pardoned if he should even relate his spiritual experiences,— if he should talk of heavenly raptures, or attribute some supernatural influence to his visionary dreams. More than this he must not do. If in the hour of trial he is conscious of a living Comforter, he must hold his peace. He may look up to heaven as steadfastly as he will; but if he see the glory of God there, and Jesus standing on the right hand of God, and if he repeat what he has seen, they will stop their ears, and run upon him with one accord, and cast him out of the city where they dwell.

But we have a right to know why it is—if God be indeed that Lord of all, in whom we live, and move and have our being—that we are to hold no conscious relations with Him. We can understand those who deny His existence altogether; however their denial may shock or distress us, we can see what it means. But to confess His power and goodness, nay, even to acknowledge His existence, and yet to separate ourselves from Him, is to act upon a principle which, in every other case, would be reckoned the greatest folly imaginable. If it were but some material force with which we had to deal, we should assuredly study its laws and manifestations: we should at least wish to have that familiarity with its operations which would enable us to avoid any evil consequences resulting from them, and to witness them without alarm. If it were a *moral* power,—some leader of thought and action, a hero or a saint,—we should watch every indication of character, try more and more to understand this lofty nature, superior indeed, yet brought within our own sphere of conduct: we should find something to imitate, something to admire; we should desire earnestly to have friendly relations with the object of our admiration, long ardently to approve ourselves in his eyes. To stand apart, refusing to look upon a noble life, busying ourselves with any trifling subject that could be employed to shut out the fair sight from our eyes,— this would be a wilful blindness which all men would condemn.

Is it, then, that we are unable to know God perfectly, and therefore that we must give up the attempt? Some such notion there is perhaps in the minds of those who set themselves in opposition nowadays to religious faith. The divisions among religious persons are so many and so grievous,—there is so little agreement even as to the fundamental articles of religion,—that it cannot be altogether a matter of surprise if lookers-on are discouraged by an apparent want of unity, and therefore of success. They will wait, they say, until the professors of divine knowledge are united among themselves, before they devote their own energies to its pursuit. Without some prospect of certainty, they have no heart to enter upon the undertaking. These things are said sometimes in all honesty; they are not always mere excuses for unbelief. Unless I am much mistaken, there is no single cause which keeps back so many from the knowledge and love of God as the variances that exist—the disputes that wake such clamorous echoes—among those who are reputed to believe and love. Would to God that we could meet the objection with a simple denial of its truth! No plea in behalf of religion would be more cogent than an argument drawn from the loving agreement everywhere to be found among Christians, and the unclouded certainty of their common faith.

But do not let us exaggerate the objection. If the human soul be indeed "athirst for God," it is nothing to the purpose to say that the thirst has often failed to lead men to the living fountain, or even that, in the very attempt to quench it, they have fallen out by the way. How many times has thirst impelled the poor victim of it to seek relief from troubled waters, or even to take some dangerous draught, rather than continue to bear his pain. The thirst was a real thirst: somewhere there was a pure stream, at which it should have been quenched, and the existence of that stream is not the less to be believed because some sufferers doubted of it, and others, wandering in their search, fell down fainting on the bye-paths they had been persuaded to take. Nay, the very thirst, not slaked, as it ought to have been, with water from the pure spring, may have weakened the man's capacity for the search; feverish, impatient excitement may have succeeded the calm, steadfast longing of health; he may be dying of thirst, yet unable to explain his need, incapable of judging what would give him true relief.

Brethren, in this matter we have much reason to take care that we do not deceive ourselves. Once we are satisfied that God has made us for Himself, and we have nothing more to do with objections. Are we prepared to deny, do we really doubt, that God is, and that He is a rewarder of them that diligently seek Him? Could we persuade ourselves for a single moment to believe that there is no existence beyond that which our bodily senses take note of? Or rather, are we not as sure of the existence of Almighty God as of our own? And would not life be intolerable if, by some strange disease in our minds, we could doubt or disbelieve its truth? Objections, then, are idle: it is too late to produce them; the cause is decided; whatever difficulties occur, we are sure that some way there must be by which they can be set at rest: if they are formidable, it is only because we have not yet viewed them aright.

It comes to this then, brethren,—that we find ourselves in the presence of God. We are not concerned with tastes or sentiments, but with a fact; we, living men, are in the presence of a living God. I ask you in all simplicity, must it not be a matter of infinite moment to us, whether we rightly perceive who this is in whose presence we stand? Must not our spiritual health, nay, our very life, depend on a right apprehension of Him, and a suitable behaviour towards Him? Let me answer in the solemn words of our Lord Himself: "This is life eternal, that they should know Thee the true God, and Jesus Christ whom Thou hast sent." To be in the presence of God and not to know it,—rather, let me say, not to know *Him*,—this is spiritual death; for it is a wilful ignorance. Above us, around us, within us, are the evidences of His presence. His Spirit "beareth witness with our spirit" that we are His children. Our hearts tell us that there is nothing hidden from Him there. In a thousand ways we have been reminded of Him; it must have been our own fault if He is not in all our thoughts. You cannot stand in the blaze of the sun's noontide heat and be unconscious of it; you may, indeed, shroud yourself in some secret place from his light and warmth, but, in the full sunshine, it is only the dead corpse that feels no influence from the ray.

Do not suppose, brethren, that I am pleading with you as with unbelievers when I thus speak. You do not deny the reality of God's presence; you have not, perhaps, even the wish to forget it: but observe, that we are all under a temptation to forget, and that even a partial forgetfulness is inconsistent with true faith. It may have happened to any one of you to find himself in a vacant room, or to have rested on a journey in what seemed a solitary place. If you suddenly became aware that there was another beside yourself in the chamber, or that the place of your rest was not as solitary as you had supposed, did you notice how your whole feeling and manner and look underwent a change? It was not that you had been doing anything for which you desired concealment, not that you had any special concern, perhaps, with the stranger of whose presence you had become aware, but that the very consciousness of not being alone has a subtle influence which no one can resist. It may be sympathy, or reserve, or courtesy, or fear,—I am not concerned to analyse the feeling; I do but recall a matter of ordinary human experience to help me to enforce the truth, that a vigorous spiritual life does not consist with even a partial forgetfulness of God.

But I am using altogether inadequate words. It is not a question of remembrance and forgetfulness; the text should have taught me better than thus to speak. The soul that lives truly to God is not content to *remember* Him; it is filled with a longing desire to enjoy His presence more and more. It is ashamed of having been so much occupied with lower thoughts. It is sensible of the meanness and vanity of this earthly life; it feels itself capable of higher things; it is vexed to be so burdened and kept down by common cares. Ever seeking to know Him better, it desires to go through life in His company, to view all things as He regards them, to choose and refuse, to love and abhor, as His guiding Spirit directs. "I am alway by Thee: for Thou hast holden me by my right hand. Thou shalt guide me with Thy counsel, and after that receive me with glory. Whom have I in heaven but Thee: and there is none upon earth that I desire in comparison of Thee. My flesh and my heart faileth: but God is the strength of my heart, and my portion for ever."

It is our desire, brethren in Christ, that these thoughts should, during this season of Lent, be brought home to your hearts. You do not deny, or wish to deny, that you are in God's presence every day. We wish you to meditate on the truth you have already confessed, to cultivate the affections that belong to it, to get your inward sight purged so as to see Him, in whom you believe, more clearly. It is in the Gospel that He will be revealed to you, not through the dull atmosphere of natural religion, but in the person of Christ, the Only-begotten Son of the Father, full of grace and truth,— a revelation which comes home to simple souls not in power only, but in sweetness, and light, and joy. We wish you to consider well what this earthly life of yours is, how lately begun, how soon to pass away; and then to set over against it the life of Him "whose goings forth have been from of old, from the days of eternity." We wish you to take the true measure of your own feebleness, and then to look upon the majestic power of the Almighty, King of kings, and Lord of lords. We would have you to meditate on His essential holiness, that you may be the more ashamed of your own defilements, more moved to desire His cleansing grace. You are cowards in your spiritual life, afraid to speak out manfully of the faith that is in you, shrinking from a comrade's laughter, fearing the ordeal of a scornful jest; you will be bolder if you think on the calm, settled purposes of God, true to His promise, steadfast in His faithfulness to irresolute, vacillating man. You find it irksome to pray, a weariness to keep the ordered round of devotion, even with its long intermissions, its large concessions to your infirmity and want of zeal. You will pray better when you have reflected earnestly on God's loving readiness to listen to your prayer. You are ever deceiving yourselves with pretences of religion, with sham motives, specious pretexts, false excuses; have you considered that there is not a word in your tongue but He knoweth it altogether? You are wilful and perverse, throwing back with strange stubbornness the love that is ever seeking to win you to itself; we wish you to dwell, in the light of the Gospel, on the depth and fulness of that divine love. Above all, we desire you, at this time of penitence, to contemplate the untiring, unbounded mercy of God, so encouraging in its offers, so beautiful in its condescension, so helpful to that personal work of repentance for sin which has to be done in every sinner's heart. And what, brethren, is to be the issue of these contemplations? Surely, as Easter draws near, you should be found in that closer communion with heavenly things which we call in the old Scripture language "walking after the Spirit," "walking by faith," "walking with God." You *cannot* think much of Him, and not wish to be much with Him. Your meditations on the poverty, and weakness, and meanness of your own condition must have been shallow indeed, if they have not made you more enamoured of the better, higher life, which is hid with Christ in God. But you will not be satisfied even then; nay, your walk with God, every step you take in it, will fill you with longings which in this world cannot be gratified to the full. Here all is imperfection, everything fragmentary, one-sided, incomplete; there only, in that future life, is the perfection which really meets the craving implanted in these souls of ours by Him who made them for Himself.

Dear brethren, I pray you be faithful to yourselves, to your better instincts, your true desires; for this is to be faithful to God from whom they come. He has not left you to yourselves. In the midst of this busy life of work, and duty, and pleasure; amidst these trials and honours, these friendships and rivalries, these sanguine hopes and passing fears, there *is* a Presence, calm steadfast, bright; a hand stretched over you to bless, a countenance so sweet that you cannot look on it and not be thankful to Him who has given you such high grace as to behold Him, though darkly, here; nor fail to pray that you may gaze upon Him in His beauty face to face.

"Beloved, now are we the sons of God, and it doth not yet appear what we shall be: but we know that when He shall appear, we shall be like Him, for we shall see Him as He is." Do not lose sight of Him now, that you may not fail to win, by His infinite mercy, that vision and that likeness in the resurrection day.

SERMON VIII.

Man's Weakness and God's Omnipotence.

2 CORINTHIANS xii. 9.

"And He said unto me, My grace is sufficient for thee: for My strength is made perfect in weakness."

THE subject appointed for our meditation to-night is thus expressed: "Man's weakness and God's omnipotence."

I think, my brethren, we shall best sustain the intention of the course, if we try, by God's help, to pursue the train of thought herein suggested in no abstract way, but in the closest relation to our faith as Christians and our need as sinners. And the text offers the best guidance; best, not only because we believe it to be inspired, but because it leads directly to the reflection that the greatest and most important illustration of the bearing of God's omnipotence upon our weakness is to be found in that revelation which alone has ever satisfied the yearning of man's helplessness for One able and willing to save.

What is this holy voice to St. Paul but the Voice of the Deliverer to lost mankind? Is it not the everlasting Gospel in a single verse? "My grace is sufficient for thee: for My strength is made perfect in weakness." And so, can we wonder that no words are dearer to the heart of Christendom, none, probably, more consulted for practical use, as men resort to a trusted friend whose advice has never failed.

The confessedly difficult context is full of interest.

St. Paul has been replying to some ungenerous religious agitators, who, not content with inventing against him charges of vacillation and priestcraft, even went so far as to allege that his "bodily presence" was "weak" and his "speech contemptible"—"annihilated outright" —such is the full sense of the word.

The holy Apostle humbly yet firmly makes his own apology in answer to these taunts. He reviews his ministry, its singleness of aim, its freedom from a mercenary motive, its ever-widening sympathies.

But, in the present chapter, he appeals to higher evidences, to the actual proofs of God's favour vouchsafed to him in certain religious experiences he had enjoyed, first through "visions and revelations," secondly through distinct support under peculiar and heavy affliction.

It would be beyond our present purpose to attempt to explain the mysterious language[a] in which the Apostle records a glorious *rapture or spiritual ecstacy* as having happened to him fourteen years before the date of this Epistle. That he had been specially favoured, like Moses and Ezekiel, with certain entrancing approaches to the very court of heaven, that he had listened to ineffable sounds, had felt translated unaccountably into regions of glory and of praise,—this, at least, we gather with some distinctness from the passage beginning: "I knew a man in Christ about fourteen years ago."

But how little more we know! Was he living in

---

[a] τινὲς δέ φασι τὰ ῥήματα πράγματα εἶναι· ἑωρακέναι γὰρ αὐτὸν τοῦ παραδείσου τὸ κάλλος, καὶ τὰς ἐν ἐκείνῳ τῶν ἁγίων χορείας, καὶ τὴν παναρμόνιον τῆς ἐμνῳδίας φωνήν. Ἀλλὰ τούτων τὴν ἀκρίβειαν αὐτὸς οἶδεν ὁ ταῦτα τεθεαμένος. Ἡμεῖς δὲ ἐπὶ τὰ συνεχῆ τῆς ἑρμηνείας βαδίσωμεν.—Theodoret, a. l.

solitude, or at Antioch with St. Barnabas? Was it after his ordination to the apostleship, or was it a gleam of divine light sent to cheer the fast and brace the soul in anxious vigil before the laying on of hands?

What follows, however, is, if possible, even more remarkable, since it suddenly unveils the private religious difficulties of the saint in the very midst of these lofty spiritual privileges.

With a frank and manly simplicity, which is ever St. Paul's characteristic habit, he here relates how, "lest" he "should be exalted above measure," there was given him a "thorn in the flesh, the messenger of Satan to buffet him."

It has been much debated what this acute trial may have been, whether some wearing and distracting pain, such as severe and prolonged headaches, according to the tradition of St. Jerome's day [b]; or whether some deep temptation of the spirit, some violent assault of passion, as teachers of the Middle Ages [c] have almost with one consent believed; or was it, as others in more recent times have (to their own satisfaction) proved, an affection of *eye-sight* illustrated by such expressions as, "Ye would have plucked out your *eyes* and given them to me [d]," and, "Ye see the size of the letters (?) in which I have written with my own hand [e];" or might it be, again, the sore trouble of false teachers piercing the holy Apostle through with many sorrows? Lastly, was

---

[b] St. Chrysostom, mentioning this idea, says, ἀλλὰ μὴ γένοιτο, and rejects the notion of any bodily ailment, believing the Apostle to refer to such adversaries as Alexander the Coppersmith.

[c] See Cornel. à Lap., Comment., a. l.

[d] Gal. iv. 15.

[e] Gal. vi. 11, πηλίκοις γράμμασιν; but cf. an interesting note appended to Dr. Lightfoot's dissertation on this subject, Ep. Gal., pp. 188-9, ed. 3, 1869.

it, as an eminent living divine and scholar prefers to think [f], some recurring epileptic or other similar seizure, incapacitating St. Paul from work for the time, rendering him, as it did our own Christian monarch Alfred the Great, altogether weak and powerless, cast down suddenly from his height of heroic energy to lie a suffering invalid under the chastening hand of God, until the attack should pass?

Certainly it is not an improper subject for reverent and cautious enquiry. Yet, brethren, how often in the sacred Scriptures where curiosity is baffled, the moral force of a passage remains unimpaired, its keen light undimmed, its practical usefulness entirely untouched by the circumstance of our ignorance!

Surely the master-truth here is *not* the *nature of the affliction*, but the contrast between the Apostle's infirmity and the infinite Power which could comfort him to the uttermost, and make his very weakness an occasion of spiritual advancement. Whatever the affliction was, its sharp agony, its prostrating weakness, its dispiriting effect on the mind, appear in the words which describe it [g]. Its victim is like a wrestler caught by an unseen arm from behind and hurled to the ground in the moment of expected victory.

A "messenger of Satan" interrupts and "buffets" him. He cries to God in prayer with the earnestness of a thrice-repeated supplication.

Oh that it might please the great Head of the Church to remove this all but intolerable hindrance to the daily work of the ministry! Oh that the same Saviour who had but now caught his soul in a divine rapture to para-

---

[f] Dr. Lightfoot, ibid.

[g] St. Chrysostom notes also the continuing distress, $κολαφίζῃ$, not $κολαφίσῃ$. See Bengel, a. l.

dise, and lifted him higher and higher to the very third heaven, would now pity his misery and mercifully remove it! But no such answer came; only a voice of far other meaning than that of release from suffering.

It is the Voice of Christ: for, be it observed, it appears from what follows to be Christ emphatically to whom St. Paul offers his prayer[h]; and so it is the Voice of Christ Jesus, that Voice from out the throne of the Ascended Humanity of the Eternal Son[i] which once before had called to Saul of Tarsus on the way to Damascus. *Then* our Lord had identified Himself with the Church in the persons of Saul's victims: "Saul, Saul, why persecutest thou *Me?*" but *now* He identifies Himself with the Church in the person of that same Saul himself: the same, yet how different! And "He said unto me, My grace is sufficient for thee: for My strength is made perfect in weakness."

Brethren, what a contrast is here! Is it not man's weakness met and corrected by the boundless and triumphant omnipotence of God? And this, not in the world of nature, but where we are more deeply, closely, personally, each of us, interested,—in the world of spirit, in life's battle, in the struggle of the mind to meet what most it dreads, most shrinks from, most longs for, power to face and to master.

We like to think of the majesty of God and the littleness of man in the world of nature. Even a thundercloud streaked for a moment with dazzling lightning, and the roar above us of heaven's artillery,—these, if they alarm with God's power, perhaps more often kindle

---

[h] Cf. Est. a. l., "Ostendit hic locus Christi fuisse verba dicentis : sufficit tibi," &c.

[i] "Ecce obiter alteram revelationem divo Paulo factam à Domino." Piconii Tripl. Expos.

thoughts of admiration and awe. But when we pass to the region of the soul, and there, amid her struggles with sin and sorrow, find the omnipotence of God in support, and comfort, and the gift of inward peace, a different sensation arises: do not we feel that this discovery of God's grace being sufficient for us is the one secret of life? Do not we feel that if we are learning, however slowly, yet surely, to know this *experience* of God's power confronting our feebleness in the secret court of conscience, then the Gospel of a suffering, sympathizing Saviour is not lost to us; we are within the folds of the saving net; we are of those to whom are still breathed from the unspeakable glory of the throne above the words of an all-powerful Friend: "My grace is sufficient for thee: for My strength is made perfect in weakness."

What, brethren, is our Lord's whole redeeming work but the omnipotence of God girding Himself with the garment of our weakness that He might succour the weak, and shew the strength of His love in this weakness?

The Shepherd leaving the ninety and nine to go after the *one lost world* is Monarch of the universe, yet a Shepherd; Almighty Lord of all lords, yet wayworn and suffering; the Light of the world, yet waiting at the heart's door as a lowly and homeless traveller! Mark how every part of His adorable life on earth illustrates this. The very weakness in which it pleased the Everlasting Son to veil His omnipotence presents the contrast at every step. Born in a manger, that same night He fills all heaven with the herald-songs of countless choirs of angels; growing up, as "a tender plant out of a dry ground," yet He answers another prophecy of the same inspired seer by being "the Mighty God, the Father of an everlasting age," hidden behind the weakness of a retired boyhood and youth at Nazareth.

Again, consider the marvellous scene of the Temptation, to which our thoughts are led at the present season. What a picture is here of God's Almighty power enabling man's natural weakness to triumph over all the armies of hell! Our Lord stands alone in the wild, unbefriended, unsupported, unarmed, as regards any visible sources of strength. He is met by the impersonation of hell's utmost power. Every conceivable temptation is concentrated and implied in the threefold assault. The lust of the flesh, the lust of the eyes, the pride of life,—appetite, covetous ambition, presumption,—what is not here included? What of the secret, what of the open assaults which had marred the life of millions for ages? Yet in vain: each poisoned shaft falls blunted from the invincible shield. It is omnipotence possessing man's weak frame in the person of the Incarnate Lord, and teaching us that, in Christ, at length our own human nature is gifted with the might of the Most High to quench all the fiery darts of the wicked one. *In Christ first*, afterwards in them that are Christ's, Christ fighting with them, Christ victorious in them,—His strength made perfect in their weakness.

We have pointed to the contrast between man's infirmity and God's ever-sufficient and boundless power. But *in Christ* we almost lose sight of the contrast in the intimate living connection. We no longer think of God's omnipotence apart from our weakness, for the one is evermore linked to the other in the heavenly chain of redeeming love.

We cannot reflect on God's infinite power without the image of Christ rising up before our thoughts, suspending at will the forces of the universe to prove His sympathy, to shew how He exerts that resistless sway to restore and comfort and save our else lost race. One moment He treads the waves of the deep lake, the next He lifts the sinking Apostle. Or He is meeting a funeral procession at Nain, and quickening to life the son of a widow. Or He is raising His own crucified and buried frame from death to life for the salvation of the world, rejoicing to reveal His perfect power in the weakness of suffering man.

Oh, my brethren! Oh, immortal yet suffering spirits! to whom I am permitted to speak to-night, what can go beyond the comfort—deep, satisfying comfort—of this revelation of the limitless power of God, whereon we may lean to the uttermost in every conceivable variety of trial, disappointment, and sorrow?

May we not, in view of this most supporting truth, apply the hymn-like words of St. Paul uttered on another occasion? "What shall we say then to these things? If God be for us, who can be against us? He that spared not His own Son, but delivered Him up for us all, how shall He not with Him also freely give us all things?.... Who shall separate us from the love of Christ? Shall tribulation, or distress?".... And again: "I can do all things through Christ which strengtheneth me [k]."

This is surely the direct and practical influence of the text on the mind of a humble and true disciple. It leads at once to the thought of the impossibility of any sorrow or temptation which can ever befal you proving more than you can meet and bear, if only you

---

[k] Rom. viii. 31, 32, 35, and Philipp. iv. 13, $ἐν\ τῷ\ ἐνδυναμοῦντί\ με$; compare this with St. Paul's use of $δύναμις$ and $δυνατός$, 2 Cor. xii. 9, 10.

lean upon the strength of Christ revealed by God's Spirit to the suffering heart.

What, then, says Christ's message to each of us but this: Do not be surprised if your trials increase, and even if the more you seem to learn the strength of God, the more you are crushed with the feeling of your own powerlessness. This is as it should be. It is thus that you are to experience the sufficiency of the power and love which made you, which died for you, which lives to sanctify you. It is thus: *not by the removal* of this or that perplexing, piercing[1] trouble, not by your release from the poverty which seems to interfere with your very religion and peace of mind, or from that bitter trial of temper which threatens to undo all Christian life and effort, or from the protracted delicacy, or recurring pain, or impending bereavement, or from anxiety about disturbing questions of opinion which agitate the Church and oppress your spirit,—not by the withdrawal of these will you learn the sufficiency of Almighty grace; but rather by their presence continually reminding you of your own weakness and need of support.

How true are the familiar lines of Edmund Waller, not of the effect of age only, but of the gradual upgrowth, as life goes on, of the knowledge of the real uses of trial:—

"The soul's dark cottage, battered and decay'd,
Lets in new light through chinks that Time hath made.
Stronger by weakness, wiser men become
As they draw nigh to their eternal home."

"Yes," says this Scripture of St. Paul to all patient and faithful hearts, "though you should be strained

---

[1] σκόλοψ, cf. LXX. Num. xxxiii. 55; Ez. xxviii. 24.

almost beyond endurance, though it be *the* trouble of all others you have always dreaded,—messenger of Satan, harassing, disheartening, perplexing, buffeting you,—yet know, O sufferer, that herein you are to feel God's power revealed to you as it never could have been without this infirmity."

Only meekly accept the trial, and it will bear this fruit "in due season" if you "faint not." Only endure the thorn, and wait,—it shall blossom as the rose.

To sum up, then, the one thought, the single precious lesson :—be our trial what it may, we are to take care lest in even wishing it altered we miss God's intended teaching for our particular case. We complain of our circumstances: we say, *This* is so trying, *that* so depressing: we wonder why, for example, *we* of all people should be marked out for this or that form of delicacy hindering us from active works of usefulness; or we fret because of some uncongenial influence in our home, and think, Ah! if it were different, *I* should be different. Or some temptation of desire, or, perchance, of intellectual doubt or restlessness about the controversies of the time,—these seem to mar our peace and make us restless and discontented; but, Oh Christian friends, if we can only recollect the watchword of the text, if we can but hide our poor wayward thoughts of self in the one deep conviction of the *sufficiency* of God, the one constant persuasion that He who tempers the "wind to the shorn lamb" will not suffer us to be tempted beyond what we are able to bear, then, but not till then, shall we discover life's greatest secret. We shall learn that Christianity is not merely a noble sentiment about a Christlike purity, nor a mere system of belief, but a life to be led for a living Person, depending on Him, loyal to Him, evermore looking to His glorified humanity as a fount of unfailing courage and patience for every sort of work and trial, if by any means we may master by lowly practice this one truth, that in Christ, by the Eternal Spirit, God's omnipotence is made perfect in our weakness.

Then, as we look out from this world of toil to the great future of futures before us, may we not hope that to us, as to one of old, will be breathed the message of assurance, "My Presence shall go with thee, and I will give thee rest?"

SERMON IX.

Man renewed in Christ, walking with God.

PSALM cxix. 57.

"Thou art my portion, O Lord."

THE subject upon which I am appointed to speak to you to-night is that of "Man renewed in Christ, walking with God." It comes as almost the closing subject of the long series of subjects, each growing out of each, which have been set before you during the Lent now closing. *To* this they have all led up; *through* this they lead up further to the concluding subject of all, viz. Man's future perfectness in the Presence of God. This circumstance defines the aspect in which I am called upon to treat of it. For look, man is not to live always in this world. He belongs to this world for time; he belongs to the next world for eternity. Here he is in the bud; there he will be in the flower and fruit. Here, at the best, he is incomplete; there he is to be made complete in whatever form of perfectness God intends for him. But, however different our condition in the other world will be, we shall be the same persons there as we are here. Yes, it will be you and I, our very selves, the self-same selves, on the other side of death and the resurrection, only that we shall be under different sets of circumstances, under different influences. Just as a tropical plant in our climate languishes, and when removed to its own climate flourishes again, but is the same plant still, though under different circumstances, so it will be with us. We shall be under different circumstances, and under new influences. So, then, the questions for us are these: What is there in that other world which is to make us perfect? and, How are we to live in this world so as to be capable of being made perfect when we come to the next?

It seems to me that men count with a strange and unreasoning confidence upon being perfectly good and holy in that future state. I suppose that there is no one in all this congregation who does not count upon it. Yet why? We know that we are not so here. Men confess that they are not what they ought to be. They say that they would like to be better, but they hardly try to be. They hear of a future world of holiness, and they put off *being* holy till they get there. They never ask themselves, What is there in that other world which is to make them complete in holiness? They never ask themselves if they are the kind of people who would be made holy by what they would find in heaven.

Suppose that God were to take us there this moment, without the trouble of dying, without the waiting for the resurrection, do you feel so very sure that what you would find there *would* render you complete and perfect?

And if not, what is to be our lot? For "without holiness no man shall see the Lord." And yet men put off the being holy until the world to come, as though *when they came there* they would be made so, as a matter of course, they know not how.

Brethren, there is that in the heaven of God which

will cause His saints to blossom into beauty inconceivable of divine holiness before His throne. There is that in the heavenly Jerusalem which will cause divine perfections to shine in and through the characters of the redeemed, as eye to eye they meet at last the Saviour whom they have seen by faith below; and in the closing sermon of this series, you will hear of what it is which shall transform the struggling sanctity of earth into the glorious perfection of the saints in bliss. It will be the actual, visible Presence of God, from out of which shall flow such strength of holiness as shall complete in every saint that which before was but struggling into bloom.

Not more surely does the returning sun of summer pour life into the struggling vegetation of winter, than the sun of God's immediate Presence shall then bring out to its completeness whatever form of half-developed sanctity the man has won his way to here. It will be the power of God's Presence that will do this. But upon whom will it have this effect? Will it have this effect upon every one? Transfer into the visible Presence of the Holy One that inhabiteth eternity a man whose every thought has been of selfish indulgence, what is there in him that should be drawn out into completed goodness? And yet men in general go on taking it for granted that they will be perfectly good in the next world, without considering whether they are the kind of people who *can* be made good by what they will find there.

Now the great work of this life is simply this, to bring us up to such a point, that when death and the resurrection are over, we may be the kind of characters to be drawn out into completed holiness by the Presence of God.

This is the work of life.

And it is just this which explains the whole outline of the Christian life, as set before us in the Church. For the whole idea of our life in the Church is based upon two main thoughts:—

(1.) That of the continual acquisition of at least a commencing holiness, commencing and ever growing here to be completed hereafter.

(2.) Of that holiness coming to us from actual contact and companionship with the Godhead now, even as it shall be completed by our closer union with the Godhead then.

Our whole spiritual life itself is but a germ from heaven planted *in* us here at baptism, which is to grow and grow until transplanted afterwards to its native heaven in the Presence of God. The *way* we grow in grace is by actual contact and companionship with Him who planted the germ of life within us; a contact and companionship veiled now, because our mortal eyesight could not bear the vision of it, but which is nevertheless only the earthly counterpart of the unveiled vision which shall make our graces bloom into glory.

Common life is but a parable of grace. Would you make a youth grow like another who is better and more resolute than himself, stronger in character, and more confirmed in goodness? You let them dwell together, live together, walk together. If there is ever so little goodness in him, it is drawn out and fostered by the companionship of the one who has more, while the evil is checked and stunted for want of anything to bring it out. We have all felt this. There is none of us but can recall times of living with some one higher-minded and nobler than we were, and how the mere living with him lifted us above ourselves; how if there were a difference between us, if we wished to do anything he disapproved of, it did not need that he should say so. We felt it. Something passed from him into us which made us *feel*, without his saying anything, what he felt upon the matter, and we were checked.

Or if we agreed with him,—if we of our own selves wished what he wished, liked what he liked, did what he approved,—why we felt as if we caught goodness from him, as if we caught steadfastness from him, as if while he was by we could even feel our conscience growing keener, our soul growing purer, our love of holiness sinking deeper, so that we came to dread the very thought of parting, as though the fountain of our strength and goodness would be withdrawn.

As if we caught goodness, did I say? Why, brethren, you know that we *do* catch goodness in this way,—that this is just the way in which we *do* catch strength and steadfastness and knowledge and purity of heart, and that as deep answers unto deep, so in very earnest soul answers unto soul, and that there is a contagion of righteousness in the communion of saints. And what is this but a parable of the ever-flowing powers of life and goodness which overflow from Him unto and into the souls of those His members who walk with Him. It is no metaphor. He *is* our life. Into those who live in Him, who walk with Him, His powers for goodness pour as by a necessary law. The sap in a tree cannot stop flowing. Because the tree lives, the sap must flow. And so because Christ is our living Head, therefore His powers for goodness and for holiness must be ever overflowing into our spiritual life. And the secret reason why, if you live with good men, their goodness steals into your life as by a spiritual electricity, is that their goodness is caught from

Christ, nay, it is Christ in them; so that it is Christ Himself who from them is passing into you, to mould your character and stimulate your graces. The spiritual man is himself in his measure a sacrament of grace, a channel of divine virtue, communicating to others that grace which has been poured into him, and so drawing you at last to Him from whom his graces came.

Why have I dwelt so long on this? For several reasons.

I. Because, like a parable, it serves to illustrate what we mean when we say that it is only by actual walking with Christ, and contact with Christ, that any good whatever is ever nurtured in us. No faith of the mere speculative intellect ever reared a single saint. Simple living with Christ, dwelling in the light of His eye, walking, acting, with Him ever at our side, and striving to do all things as He would have done them, had He been in our place; this rears thousands into sanctity who never know that they are saints. By this the germ of our renewed life is fostered, its powers stimulated, its growth developed. By this our commencing holiness is kept increasing, so that it may be ready to burst into its completed bloom when we shall be transferred at last, risen and exalted, to the Presence of the Lord. As the Sacrament of the Holy Eucharist is the counterpart of the adoration of the Lamb, so the walk with Christ on earth is the rehearsal of, and the preparation for, the life with God in heaven.

II. Second reason. Because in actual practice this is the actual way in which most men *are* led up to the walk with God on earth; and it is most important to notice God's providential order as a guide and suggestion for our own practice. Nothing is more important than for the guide of souls to study God's ways and strive to follow out His perfect guidance. And so we note the fact that, practically, in a large majority of cases, Christ does not draw men to Him by His own immediate action. Sometimes He does. We all of us have seen cases of it; history tells of many; holy Scripture shews us more. Still, for every Saul converted by the overt action of the Lord Himself, there is many a Philip led by his brother Andrew. So the usual case is that He acts on us through His members, and through His Church. When first we walk with Him, we are unconscious that it is He that we are walking with. Some good man's life, some saintly woman's companionship, has cast its spell of divine attraction over us. They draw us to them, we walk with them, we cannot help being drawn nearer and nearer, and the magic of spiritual forces influences and moulds us. At first, we scarcely see or know what power it is we yield to. At last our spiritual eyes begin to open, and we learn that there is in them a divine life working, which gives them their supernatural magnetic power over us, and then we are led *ourselves* to seek the same divine companionship which has made them what they are.

III. And, then, thirdly, if this be so, what a prodigious argument it is why, in all our arrangements respecting the life and culture of those whom we are set to teach and guide and govern, we should provide to the uttermost that they should be placed within the sphere of the supernatural influences which flow forth from the lively members of Christ's Body. What a value does this set upon the religious element in all places and systems of education. Not that the young themselves are at the moment conscious of it. Perhaps the less so the better. All vital processes go on almost unconsciously. The moment you begin to feel them, there is something wrong. So we would train our youth amid men of spiritual mould, and daily services and frequent Eucharists, channels of His grace and Presence; that as their soul's eye opens upon life and responsibility, it may rest at once on Him who walketh amid the seven golden candlesticks, that they may then take Him for their guide in life, and walk with Him in preparation for the eternal Presence, which is the bliss of eternity. Aye, and not only so. For remember that this is not only the bliss of eternity, but that this is the very object for which God created man, and unto which He would have *all* men come. Heaven, and the joy of heaven, sanctity and the bliss of holiness, is not a thing apart, which God has devised for a chosen few as favoured darlings of His grace. Not so. The heights of heaven were *meant* for all, and they will be for all who will but seek them, even as His grace is freely offered to all who will walk with Him here. No soul here to-night but has been "renewed in Christ" by the power of the Holy Ghost. No soul here but may be walking through life with Christ his Lord, and catching heavenly tempers from that divine companionship each day that he "walks with God." No soul, therefore, but may in the dawn of the Resurrection, rise to the full fruition of the companionship which budded here, and in the long ages of eternity develope in limitless expansion the ever-growing sanctities which shall be fostered in those who shall be "for ever with the Lord." Amen.

Printed by James Parker and Co., Crown-yard, Oxford.

www.ingramcontent.com/pod-product-compliance
Lightning Source LLC
Chambersburg PA
CBHW020058170426
43199CB00009B/320